Sourcebook for Children with
Attention Deficit Disorder
Second Edition

A Management Guide for Early Childhood Professionals and Parents

With Reproducible Handouts in English and Spanish

Clare B. Jones, Ph.D.

Illustrations by
Cathie Lowmiller

Communication Skill Builders®
a division of
The Psychological Corporation
555 Academic Court
San Antonio, Texas 78204-2498
1-800-228-0752

Reproducing Pages from This Book

As described below, some of the pages in this book may be reproduced for instructional use (not for resale). To protect your book, make a photocopy of each reproducible page. Then use that copy as a master for photocopying.

The book is dedicated to my late parents,
who encouraged me to be an author,
and to Doug and Lindsay,
who helped make that dream come true.

About the Author

Clare Banker Jones received the Ph.D. in education from the University of Akron with cognates in early childhood and gerontology. A diagnostic specialist, she is certified to teach children who have learning disabilities and mental handicaps, as well as children in a regular classroom. She is a validator for the National Association for the Education of Young Children. In 1985, Dr. Jones was honored by the Martha Holden Jennings Foundation as a Master Teacher in Ohio. That year, the United States Department of Aging named her program, *Grandparent Reads to Me,* the best intergenerational program in the nation. As a classroom teacher, she was selected in Ohio to be a VIP visiting professor at Cleveland State University. In 1992, she was named by the California Association of Resource Specialists as Community Educator of the Year. A special educator/early childhood teacher and administrator since 1967, she has taught every level of special education, preschool to high school.

Dr. Jones is the former Director of Education at Phoenix Children's Hospital; and has been a faculty associate at Arizona State University, Northern Arizona University, and Glendale Community College. She operates a private practice in Phoenix.

Publications by Clare B. Jones

Also published by Communication Skill Builders, a division of The Psychological Corporation:

> *Attention Deficit Disorder: Strategies for School-Age Children*

> *Young and Active: Strategies for Elementary Students with ADHD*
> (videotape)

Contents

Reproducible Pages

Preface

Sourcebook for Children with Attention Deficit Disorder: A Management Guide for Early Childhood Professionals and Parents, published in 1991, was so well received by the educational community that in 1997 revision was deemed necessary. When I wrote the *Sourcebook,* it was one of the nation's first titles in the area of attention deficit disorder; now, there are several hundred. However, as of the date of this writing, the *Sourcebook* remains the only book totally dedicated to early childhood attention disorders.

I am grateful for the response of readers everywhere to the *Sourcebook.* Over the years, I have received many letters from teachers, parents, and therapists who read the book. I am honored by the people who come to my workshops across the country bringing their well-worn copies for me to autograph. As an author, there is no greater experience.

I am especially proud of this revised edition, which includes handouts and take-home sheets for parents who are Spanish-speaking. I have retained all the original activities for the classroom because, like all good teaching strategies, they are timeless.

I personally want to thank the people who helped to make this revision of the *Sourcebook* a reality. They include my acquisitions editor, Pat Zureich, and my typist, Joanne Howell.

My practice now includes nine colleagues, and I see children on a weekly basis. The children and families I see every day continue to inspire me and help me to grow as a professional. I have reduced my adjunct teaching role at the university to allow time to present workshops and inservices across the United States. In my travels, I have met a wonderful group of professionals and parents whose support and interest has been so rewarding to me.

My husband, Doug, continues to be my first and best editor and my closest friend. My daughter, Lindsay, who is now in graduate school, has grown up hearing her name used in my workshops and seeing her name in my books. I use her name to protect the actual client's identity. My only explanation is that as I write and work she is constantly in my thoughts and in my heart.

The field of attention deficit continues to be a critical area in mental and neurobehavioral health and part of the lives of countless children in the world. No one chooses to have attention deficit, but many parents and professionals who read this book choose to serve, help, and honor these children. For that, I will always be grateful.

The terms *attention deficit* and initials *ADD* and *ADHD* are interchangeable and are used this way throughout the text.

If we are to teach real peace in this world and if we are to carry on a real war against war, we shall have to begin with children: and if they will grow up in this natural innocence, we won't have to struggle: we won't have to pass fruitless, idle resolutions, but we shall go from love to love and peace to peace, until at last all the corners of the world are covered with that peace and love for which, consciously or unconsciously, the whole world is hungering.

– Mahatma Mohandas K. Gandhi
November 18, 1931

. . . and a little child shall lead them.

– Isaiah 11:6

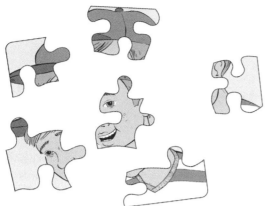

Chapter 1

Introduction to Attention Deficit Disorder

Mike is a bright-eyed, spunky six-year-old who runs into me full force as I enter his first grade classroom during story time. "Hey, teacher!" he yells. "Look what just walked into our room—a space cadet!" I turn to the teacher, whose interrupted story time is now evolving into chaos. She smiles patiently. "Hello, Dr. Jones," she says. "I guess I don't have to point out Mike to you now. You two have just met personally!"

In my role as an educational consultant, I have been asked to observe the *very* young man who collided into me at the door. The teacher skillfully handles my well-announced entrance and gently draws the class back to the story she was reading. I find an out-of-the-way spot in the room and turn my own attention to the children as they listen to the tale of an adventurous rabbit. As the teacher employs her strong style to make the story come alive, the children sit in rapture—*most* of the children, that is, except Mike. He is now sitting off to the side of the group, spinning like a top and singing to himself. Mike's teacher and parents have asked me to spend a day learning more about him because they are concerned about his overactive, distracted, and often impulsive nature. They feel he is a bright child who is behind his peers in attention, learning, and self-control.

In an early childhood classroom, we expect a certain amount of active, energetic behavior and consider it part of normal, developmentally appropriate behavior. But at a certain age, children are expected to begin showing signs of learning self-control so that their behavior is better balanced by the time they finish the early elementary grades. Self-control is an essential skill that helps children focus their energy and attention on their role in school, which is primarily learning. This challenge with self-control observed in Mike is what is so singularly disconcerting to those who care for him.

There are some children who are so easily distracted and overstimulated by their environment that they respond with a consistent pattern of inattentiveness, impulsivity, and excessive physical activity. These essential features collectively form the basis of attention deficit disorder.

What Is Attention Deficit Disorder?

Attention deficit is a disorder that affects children from the first months of their lives through their school years, through adolescence, and into adulthood. The degree to which it affects the child will vary by individual and environment, but it is a lifelong disorder. It is characterized by symptoms of inattention, impulsivity, and hyperactivity at levels that are considered maladaptive and inappropriate for a child's age or stage of normal development. These three areas can affect how the person functions throughout early childhood in school, in social situations, in the family, and in the workplace. For more than half of the people diagnosed with attention deficits, the American Psychiatric Association's *Diagnostic and Statistical Manual of Mental Disorders (DSM-IV)* (1994) places the onset of the disorder before age seven. About 40% of the diagnosed population show symptoms that persist into adulthood.

The *DSM-IV,* a classification system written by psychologists and psychiatrists, lists all the disorders for which professionals provide treatment. Descriptions in the *DSM-IV* that include three diagnostic subtypes of the disorder are classified based on a predominance of either inattention or hyperactive-impulsive symptoms. The term *Attention Deficit/Hyperactivity Disorder (ADHD)* includes specific criteria to identify inattentive impairment and two hyperactivity subsets: hyperactive and impulsive. An individual can be classified as having either an inattentive type or hyperactive-impulsive type of attention deficit disorder. If both symptoms are present, then the diagnosis is a combined type.

The disorder occurs more frequently in males than in females. On the average, male children are between 2.5 and 5.6 times more likely than female children to be defined or diagnosed as having ADHD within epidemiological samples of children, with the average being three boys to one girl (Lewinsohn, et al. 1993; Barkley and Mash 1996). More males are diagnosed with the hyperactive-impulsive symptoms than females. For children diagnosed with the hyperactive symptoms, the height of their hyperactivity appears to be between the ages of two and eight years, followed by a tapering of the symptoms where the child appears to be more restless than active. This change in observed activity level often leads people to believe that children "grow out of" hyperactivity when, in actuality, they are really learning to cope with it; they are not as *physically* out of control.

Each child with an attention disorder is unique, but these children have common characteristics or anomalies that clearly identify them as having the disorder. Along with the three essential features that involve short attention span, impulsivity, and hyperactivity, these children also may exhibit difficulties with short-term memory, visual motor integration, insatiability, inconsistent performance, and social difficulties. At times, a discrepancy exists between intellectual ability and actual productivity. Children with ADHD often exhibit a lack of production rather than an inability to learn. Many children with the disorder tend to be described as daydreamers. They are disorganized; they have difficulty starting and finishing a task with a group; transitions are challenging for them. Parents and teachers begin to observe a pattern of inconsistent work of unacceptable quality. Interpersonal relationships will be a challenge to some children with attention deficit because they have a hard time waiting, delaying their impulses, and sustaining consistent interest; and overall they have a general insensitivity to feedback cues. The difficulty they may experience with concentration and memory often impedes their ability to understand social prediction (the sequential flow in social context). Their social interactions are too often marked by fighting, verbal interruption, and, eventually, social rejection. They may have low self-esteem because of this rejection.

Of the 15 characteristics in the *DSM-IV* definition criteria, "(2) (a), Often fidgets with hand or feet or squirms in seat" is the behavior most frequently reported in the National Field Trials of the Descriptive Criteria (American Psychiatric Association 1994). Children who do not experience the hyperactivity component of the diagnosis tend to be overly passive, lethargic, and somewhat anxious. They tend to have a flat, affective style. Children who have attention deficit disorder without hyperactivity generally are quiet and have a timid, rather unassuming social style. They frequently go unnoticed in school, and they are generally withdrawn rather than presenting behavior problems. They are often described as "unmotivated" or "immature." See table 1 for a listing of some of the specific behavior of each diagnosis.

TABLE 1
Attention deficit disorder: A comparison

ADHD Inattentive	ADHD Hyperactive-Impulsive
Often an easy, mellow baby	Often hard to console, colicky as baby
Tends to have lower verbal interaction	Excessive talking
Daydreamer	Physically active
Greater difficulty paying attention to the main aspects of a task	Difficulty staying on tasks and completing them
Often forgetful in daily activities	Difficulty waiting for turns
Seems unmotivated at times	Excessively impatient
OR, A COMBINATION OF BOTH	

Historical Overview

The study of different levels of behavior in children began in the late eighteenth century. At that time, medical researchers noted symptoms of in-attention and hyperactivity in children recovering from certain types of insult to the brain, such as infections of the central nervous system and head injury (Ebaugh 1923). Through the twentieth century, researchers continued investi-gating abnormal behavior levels and relating them to indications of brain damage. As a result, this type of disorder was labeled with a variety of terms that implied a neurological origin, including *minimal brain dysfunction, hyper-kinetic syndrome,* and *brain damage syndrome.* Educators in the 1950s and 1960s used the words *hyperactive, hyperkinetic,* and *minimal brain damage* in their studies of these behaviors and of learning difficulties and motor-perceptual dysfunction. In the 1970s, psychologists and psychiatrists throughout the nation formulated a classification system of all disorders for which they provide treat-ment. The resulting *Diagnostic Statistical Manual of Mental Disorders (DSM)* labeled the behavior as "Attention Deficit with or without Hyperactivity" and marked the first attempt to define the disorder according to specific criteria. This label was changed in the third edition of the *DSM* (1987), and the most current *DSM-IV* (1994) changed the label again. The term used now, *Attention Deficit Disorder,* is expressed as Attention Deficit/Hyperactivity Disorder with a slash indicating with or without hyperactivity.

Possible Causes

Research regarding the causes of ADD/ADHD remains inconclusive, but there is strong evidence linking the condition to genetic, prenatal, environmental, or physical factors. Studies of children with attention deficit reveal that they generally have noticeable behavior differences from birth (Wender 1987).

Current clinical research supports the hypothesis that altered brain biochemistry is a factor in attention disorders. Dr. Judith Rapoport, chief of the Child Psychiatry Branch at the National Institute of Mental Health in Bethesda, Maryland, has been exploring this research with the use of magnetic resonance imaging (MRI) to study the brain anatomy of children with attentional concerns (1995). Based on neuropsychology studies at NIH, Rapoport found clear differences between the brains of children who have attention disorders and those who do not. Researchers noted that parts of the anterior frontal lobe and the basal ganglia were smaller, particularly on the right side. Boys identified in the testing with attention disorder show a statistically significant difference in an important structure of the brain. The boys in the sample with attention disorders lacked a larger right-side brain as seen in "normal specimens." In earlier research at the National Institute of Mental Health, Alan Zametkin and his research team using the PET Scan (positron emission tomography machine) were able to show that the rate at which the brain uses glucose, its main energy source, was lower in subjects with hyperactivity of childhood onset as compared with normal subjects. They report these specific findings in the *New England Journal of Medicine* (November 1990), and their research is continuing today. Zametkin and his researchers have determined that the frontal lobes of the brain are involved in regulating attention, emotional responses, and activity level. Further, the frontal lobes play a role in planning, an area in which children with attention disorders typically have great difficulty. Rapoport's research includes the function of the basal ganglia. In any cerebral function that involves some sort of response inhibition, the basal ganglia often comes into play, as it does in the planning of complex sequences of actions. Hence, both Zametkin's and Rapoport's research conclusively demonstrates that neurotransmitters play a role in behavior concentration and impulsivity.

Research is extending to understand the role of dopamine in the brain's braking system. Dopamine is a neurotransmitter, or messenger molecule. Simply stated, dopamine allows one neuron in the brain to talk to another. Dr. F. X. Castellanos has suggested that high levels of dopamine metabolites in the cerebrospinal fluid (fluid that protects the brain and spinal cord) correlated with high degrees of hyperactivity in 29 boys. He noted that dopamine is developmentally active and that its concentration in cerebrospinal fluid peaks at about the age of two and declines rapidly over the next dozen years. It is an interesting coincidence that younger children with ADHD appear to have an "excess of the particular neurotransmitter that facilitates exploration of their environment and that the concentrations of this substance would generally decrease as children become older and less adventurous" (Castellanos 1997, 32). This ongoing research is certainly important in beginning to understand the levels of attention disorder.

Prevalence

Attention deficit is one of the more frequent childhood disorders, and it is the single most common reason why children are referred to child mental health clinics today (Barkley 1981). The high prevalence of attention deficit disorder suggests that no teacher will ever teach again without having at least one child with attention deficit in the classroom. The most commonly cited figures (a conservative estimate) show that attention deficits occur in 1% to 6% of children (Lambert, Sandoval, and Sassone 1978). Shaywitz and Shaywitz (1991) suggest that attention deficits affect 10% to 20% of the school–age population. A survey of more than 2,000 third and fourth graders in Arizona (Hepworth, Jones, and Sehested 1991) found a prevalence of 14%. With a disorder that has the range of causes that this one appears to have, we are bound to see a population of significant size.

For more than half the people diagnosed with attention deficit disorder, the *DSM-IV* definition places the onset no later than age seven, and symptoms may persist into adulthood. Boys tend to be diagnosed before the age of eight, while girls tend to be diagnosed later in life. It is a consistent finding that girls are more frequently diagnosed with attention deficit disorder inattentive type than attention deficit disorder hyperactive/impulsive type. Attention deficit varies in severity and the degree to which it affects children who have it. Some children have great difficulty with overactivity. Other children experience severe concentration difficulties but little overactivity. See table 2 for a listing of the criteria for grading severity of ADHD.

TABLE 2
Criteria for grading severity of attention deficit/hyperactivity disorder

Mild	Few, if any, symptoms in excess of those required to meet the diagnosis and no or minimum impairment in school and/or social functioning
Moderate	Symptoms of functional impairment ranging between *mild* and *severe*
Severe	Many symptoms in excess of those required to make the diagnosis, plus significant and pervasive impairment in function at home, in school, and with peers

Reproduced with permission from the *Diagnostic and Statistical Manual of Mental Disorders, Third Edition–Revised.* Copyright 1987 American Psychiatric Association.

Treatment and Solutions: What Works?

Research indicates that the most effective form of management is a multi-modality intervention that includes medical management; parent training; individual, group, and family psychotherapy; and interventions aimed at improving school performance. One of the biggest hurdles faced by practitioners, parents, and individuals with ADHD is simply the fact that there is no single right answer. It is true that our knowledge about the disorder, research, and how to treat it is expanding dramatically, but attention deficit disorder remains a multi-faceted challenge to everyone. The components suggested in table 2 are to be considered by the parent and physician as they plan a treatment program for the child. If we respect that each child is unique, then a treatment plan for each child must be unique. Children's individual treatment plans are determined by their physical status, their genetic background, the severity of their symptoms, and other considerations. The strategies listed in "What Works" (see pages 7 and 8) are frequently effective with the child who has attention disorders. They are not listed in any specific order.

Treatment for attention deficit disorder must involve multimodality intervention. When it does, the improvement can be dramatic.

What Works

These strategies are not listed in any specific order.

- *Family understanding of attention disorder*
  Parent training, counseling, and support

- *Behavior therapy*
  Consistent behavior intervention based on positive reinforcement and mixing group and individual rewards; the use of *response cost* (that is, losing tokens for undesirable behavior)

- *A healthy sense of self-esteem*
  Experiences of success in which peer and family response to the child is positive and immediate. Finding an area of success, possibly outside of academic achievement

- *Medical interventions*
  Drug therapy is a short-term treatment. Medication may be just one component in the treatment plan

- *Educational interventions*
  Appropriate educational accommodations provided by knowledgeable teachers and multidisciplinary teams

- *Counseling*
  Training in social skills, coping skills, new goal-directed strategies

Lo Que Sí Funciona

Las siguientes estrategias no aparecen en orden de importancia.

• **Comprensión familiar de déficit de atención**
Programas de entrenamiento, consejo y apoyo para los padres.

• **Terapia del comportamiento**
Intervención en cuanto al comportamiento, basada en el sistema de refuerzo y recompensa tanto individual como comunal. El use de "costo de conducta" (en el cual el comportamiento no-apropiado cuesta fichas).

• **Un sentido sano de amor propio**
Cuando familiares y compañeros responden al niño de manera positiva e inmediata, el niño siente éxito. Encontrar algo que puede hacer bién, no necesariamente en el área de logros academicos.

• **Intervenciones médicas**
Los medicamentos se usan por corto plazo. Representan sólo una parte del programa de tratamiento.

• **Intervención escolar**
Modificaciones apropiadas basadas en las recomendaciones de maestros y equipos multidisciplinarios.

• **Psicoterápia**
Programas de entrenamiento para comportamiento socialmente aceptable, destrezas para enfrentarse a las malas situaciones, y estrategias para alcanzar metas.

Medication

One of the most controversial parts of the multimodality intervention plan is the use of psychostimulant medication. Stimulant drug therapy as a short-term tactic, however, is perceived as highly effective. Barkley (1997) notes a success rate of 96% for students diagnosed as ADHD hyperactive-impulsive type, and a success rate of 70% for those diagnosed as ADHD inattentive.

The most commonly prescribed stimulants are Ritalin® (methylphenidate hydrochloride), Dexedrine® (D-amphetamine), and Adderall® (single-entity amphetamine). Cylert® (pemoline) was also used, but in 1997 an FDA warning cautioned many practitioners against it. The first three stimulants are termed *rapid acting* because they produce effects within 45 minutes after ingestion, and the effects peak within three to four hours. Because of their fast-acting, fast-exiting effects, they are often prescribed two or three times daily. They are available in time-released format.

Any treatment program using medication must be monitored carefully through periodic follow-up visits to a physician and the distribution of observation guidelines and checklists for recognizing side effects to all adults who have significant contact with the child. Parents and their children need to be made aware of the purpose of the medication, its side effects, and the reason why it is being considered. It is also important to know what medication does not do:

1. It does not make this child smarter. If the child's performance increases in school, it is probably because of productivity. The child is producing more work; the child is able to concentrate, attend, and complete tasks.

2. It does not make the child socially acceptable. Characteristics of attention deficit disorder include impulsivity and aggressiveness. Because of these behaviors, this child is often not accepted in many social circles. Medication does not increase social competence. Therefore, the parents or school continually will have to provide additional modeling in social skills, social strategies, and social interactions.

3. The medication does not change the child's moods. If the child is depressed or anxious, a psychostimulant will not remedy this. If the child is now feeling more successful, thanks to academic production, perhaps the child's self-esteem will increase; but this does not relate to social withdrawal or an overall happier mood.

4. It does not make the child into a zombie or a robot. While taking medication, the child will not *automatically* do things that he or she has not previously learned or understood.

Once a child is on medication and is more focused, it is a key time for teachers and parents to review rules or past information the student has not learned. Children with ADHD may have gaps in their educational history. It would be helpful if these ignored skills could be retaught once a child is on medication. The skill level may increase now that more modeling is apparent.

In their book, *Beyond Ritalin* (1996), Garber, Garber, and Spizman state, "Attention Deficit Disorder is a complex disorder. It cannot simply be cured by a pill. It is crucial for youngsters and adults with ADHD, their loved ones, and those who work with them to understand what effect medication may have on the troubling characteristics of the disorder. If they are allowed to use medication, they must realize it is never the sole form of treatment, and they must make a commitment to identify and work to control, cope with, or solve those problems that medication alone simply cannot solve" (10).

Behavior Therapy

Psychotherapy, often considered in a multimodality approach, is used with children who need guidance and understanding of their behaviors. The technique of *self-talk* therapy (teaching children to monitor their inner covert speech) as a form of behavior management is a successful tool for some. Goals for therapy can include learning eye contact, appropriate social greetings, and appropriate interaction during playtime. Individual or peer-group counseling also may benefit some children in repairing their self-esteem or overcoming feelings of depression.

Self-Esteem

ADHD children benefit from being involved in activities outside of school or the day-care environment in which they can develop a strong sense of self-worth. Several studies indicate that children who have coped well with attention deficit have had a long-term history of being successful in a specific activity. Generally, it is a noncompetitive physical activity such as swimming, tennis, drama, or horseback riding. The martial arts is an area that can be helpful for children with ADHD. In martial arts, children learn sequential skills, honor for self, and control in unmonitored situations. Encouraging children to participate in community social activities such as "Mom and Me" exercise classes, play groups, or library story hours also can help them to develop social skills and build confidence in entering new situations.

Educational Interventions

Educational interventions are a very significant part of a multimodality treatment. Children with ADHD generally spend the majority of their time in a regular mainstreamed classroom. It is in this setting that they acquire the bulk of their academic and social-interaction skills. It is important that the classroom teacher understands the strengths and weaknesses of these children and is able to implement sound educational strategies within the learning environment. By learning about each child's unique needs, the teacher can assist with behavior control which, in turn, will help the teacher feel more successful. In subsequent chapters, we will examine positive classroom interventions for the challenging student, and the roles of the teacher and other professionals in employing these techniques.

Characteristics

The essential characteristics of attention deficit disorder—inattention, impulsivity, and hyperactivity—exist, in one form, in both the inattentive and hyperactive-impulsive child. The hyperactivity characteristic can be explained best by the activity level of the child. However, children with inattentive symptoms should be thought of as children whose brains are hyperactive, although their bodies may not be.

The following three descriptions give us a closer look at inattention, impulsivity, and hyperactivity.

Inattention
"Huh? What did you say?"

These children have difficulty focusing and concentrating on stimuli presented. At times, their concentration will appear to be quite focused and clear, yet easily diverted. Parents often report that their child can spend an hour playing with one toy (for example, interlocking plastic building blocks or a video game), but is unable to attend long enough to follow directions at the dinner table. They describe their child as "tuning out" or "daydreaming" at certain times. The children themselves explain their behavior in terms like these: "My brain takes a snooze"; "My eyes keep going out the window"; or "I have radar ears."

The symptoms of attention deficit are diverse in their presentation. Some children are particularly distracted by visual stimuli, such as movement or color. Others are distracted by auditory stimuli—unusual noises and background sounds. Activities requiring sustained attention are the most challenging for all children with attentional problems.

Impulsiveness
"He did what?!!!"

These children have difficulty thinking before they act. They appear to act without planning or thinking about the consequences. They may blurt out a response before thoroughly understanding the question, or they may interrupt a conversation to share information that has no bearing on the topic. In one instance, when a boy on the playground made a funny face, a child with ADD reached out and slapped him. When later asked by the teacher about what occurred, the child had no idea what happened. In another example, a child with ADD was coloring an art project enthusiastically when suddenly she threw her crayon aside and tore up her artwork. When questioned later, she could only repeat, "I didn't like it." This impulsive style leads to difficulty in completing the task. As children with ADD get older, they will have difficulty with details and often will demonstrate inaccuracies in math and spelling, two academic areas that demand keen attention to detail. Impulsiveness leads to problems with organizing materials, assignments, and information. These children appear messy, unsure, and forgetful. They may frequently call out in class, otherwise interrupt, or find it hard to wait for their turn in group activities. They often appear tired or bored when pressured to complete a long task requiring concentration.

Hyperactivity

Tap, wiggle, fuss, fidget!

These children constantly play with paper clips, rubber bands, toy cars, or pencils. They tap their fingers on the desk, wiggle, and shake their feet and legs. Many teachers describe these children as "always on the go." Preschool teachers often say that they are worn out from keeping up with these bundles of energy. Parents report that the overactivity during the day doesn't stop at night; their children are restless sleepers who toss, turn, and call out in their sleep. Classroom teachers report that these children often tap on their desks or otherwise disrupt the class. The teachers ask the children to stop, but several minutes later the children begin again. Such constant activity is seldom goal directed and appears random or purposeless. Parents state that when these children become mobile, they immediately begin to challenge their environment, jumping from the crib and attempting to climb barriers. Parents in support groups often swap "war stories" about the physical feats their children attempted before the age of four.

Other Characteristics

In addition to these three essential features, other characteristics may be noted, including emotional instability, difficulty interacting with peers, and inconsistent performance. Coupled with a child's attention deficit may be disabilities in the areas of memory, perceptual function, language, and sequential tasks. A learning disability also may be present; it is believed that between 15% to 20% of children and adults with learning disabilities also have attention deficits (Silver 1990; Weiss 1990).

Understanding Strengths and Weaknesses

When we look at the characteristics of attention deficit disorder, we tend to look at the weaknesses or the areas we perceive as dysfunctional. To constructively compensate for or alter the weakness, first we need to understand the child's strengths. With this information, we can predict what the child does and use it to help him or her cope with the weaker areas. In his book, *On Playing a Poor Hand Well* (1997), Dr. Mark Katz points out that children with attentional concerns are very resilient. They often respond to adversity and challenges with good spirit and fortitude. The strengths in children with attention disorders vary just as individuals vary, but these strengths tend to cluster in some basic observable characteristics. They include:

Visual Gestalt Skills. Visual gestalt is simply the ability to see the "big picture" quickly. Children with this strength see the whole picture, "the cover on the book," and quickly determine what has occurred or will occur. They easily interpret others' feelings by their expressions and body language and often react based on their immediate impression.

Long-Term Memory. Children of this particular strength often are able to recall and accurately report particular events and unique experiences that occurred years before. One mother shared a story with me involving her daughter. As they passed an office building one day, her daughter said, "Mom, there's that building where we saw that lady wearing the silver boots. Remember? We stopped by here to see Aunt Connie, and the lady was in the lobby." That incident had occurred two years prior. Recently, while observing one of my clients in school, I heard him say to his teacher, "Mrs. Smith, you wore that cowboy blouse last year to the basketball assembly. I saw you when I was in second grade."

Creativity, Inventiveness, and Imagination. Children with attention disorders often have particular creativity with great imagination. They are able to describe events with intense emotion and vigor. Their oral descriptions of how they lost their homework assignments can excite an audience! Parents and teachers are impressed with their wide variety of ideas and their range of responses.

Unusual Application of Higher-Level Skills. Often observed in mathematics applications, this ability to quickly interpret simultaneous thinking is a definite strength. The child may miss basic calculation steps, but understand the higher application process of the problem.

Verbal Expression. Another strength of these students tends to be verbal expression skills. They can speak at length about topics freely, adding other subjects to the initial topic as they speak. Their conversation can be exciting, multifaceted, and dynamic.

Conversely, we must examine some of the areas that challenge these children. Although they have the capacity to see the big picture quickly (whole gestalt), they overlook the details and sequential steps of a task. In preschool and kindergarten experiences, it takes them longer to memorize the alphabet and learn the names of colors. While their conversations are engaging and lively, they may not listen to others. They appear almost egocentric, more interested in themselves than in others past normal development stages. Their long-term memory skills enable them to develop a background of cumulative events, but their short-term memory skills are weaker and make day-by-day tasks more difficult. They can remember everything you want to know about the history of Nintendo®, but they can't remember to put their names on their papers in class. They're challenged by work that is rote, tedious, or sequential in nature, requiring detail or careful scrutiny. They become bored easily; yet they are often compassionate, curious, and most enthusiastic about areas in which they have been successful.

Children with attention disorders often are at high risk for a number of challenges in areas of performance related to cognitive function relative to their own-age peers. In the book, *ADHD in the Schools,* written by George DuPaul and Gary Stoner (1994), the authors relate that on the average, children with attention disorders do not differ from the rest of the school population in regard to intellectual functioning. They point out that this disorder does not appear to affect their general cognitive abilities. They do see that children with attention deficit evidence difficulties in problem solving, organizational skills, expressive language abilities, and fine or gross motor control. Although, as a group, children with attention deficit are at greater-than-average risk for language, motor control, and problem-solving difficulties, many children with this disorder *do not* exhibit these problems. These are children who have academic underachievement problems, gifted children with attention deficit, and children with attention deficit who are experiencing conduct disorder or behavior adjustment problems.

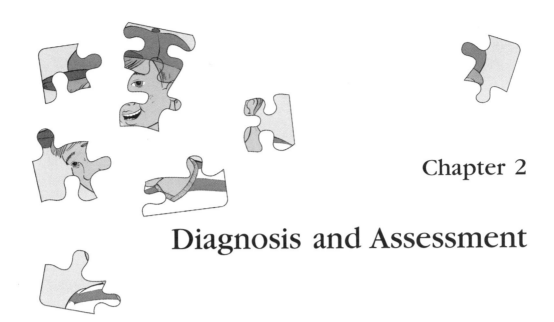

Chapter 2

Diagnosis and Assessment

Because normally developing preschoolers tend to be highly active, attention deficit or hyperactivity is often difficult to diagnose at an early stage. However, it is important to note that it is a strong hereditary disorder. Thus, many of the beginning characteristics will be observed by the family and can be seen in the developing child. Even when it is obvious to everyone around the child that something is wrong, the line between extremes of normal development and behavior and symptoms of a disorder may be unclear. "The terrible twos" describes the stage at which most two-year-olds experience bouts of inattention, egocentricity, and single-channeled child behaviors. These behaviors hardly seem to differ from the overall descriptive guidelines in the *DSM-IV*. Further, the child's behavior is likely to change unpredictably throughout the day, going from periods of intense activity to relative calm. The diagnosis of ADHD needs to be made by an experienced developmental practitioner who understands these dilemmas and recognizes that the symptoms of behavior problems are more overt, more intense, and more serious than age-appropriate behaviors. A practitioner needs to have a full understanding of the normal development of attention and its implications for learning.

Normal Development of Attention Control

It is important, therefore, that practitioners be extremely familiar with the range of normal developmental milestones of the attention span and begin to compare which stage seems most appropriate to the child they are working with. Through these observations, clinicians may develop hypotheses about the child's attention span to be followed up during more formal assessments.

Cooke and Williams (1987) outline six levels of normal development and attention control based on research by Jean Reynell (1980). These levels may be used to assess the child's development of attention skills.

Level I (Birth to One Year). Level I is characterized by extreme distractibility, in which children's attention shifts from one object, person, or event to another. Any new event (such as someone walking by or another child entering the room) will immediately distract these children.

Level II (One to Two Years). Children in Level II can concentrate on a concrete task of their own choosing, but will not tolerate any visual or verbal intervention from an adult. These children may appear obstinate or stubborn; but, in fact, their attention is single-channeled. They must ignore all extraneous stimuli in order to concentrate upon the task at hand.

Level III (Two to Three Years). Children's attention is still single-channeled in Level III. They cannot attend to competing auditory and visual stimuli from different sources. For example, they cannot listen to an adult's direction while playing; although, with the adult's help, they can shift their full attention to the speaker and then back to the game.

Level IV (Three to Four Years). Children in Level IV must still alternate full attention (visual and auditory) between the speaker and the task, but now do this spontaneously without an adult needing to focus that attention.

Level V (Four to Five Years). By Level V, attention is two-channeled; that is, these children understand verbal instructions related to the task without interrupting the activity to look at the speaker. Their concentration span still may be short, but brief instruction is possible.

Level VI (Five to Six Years). In the final stage, auditory, visual, and manipulatory channels are fully embedded, and attention is well established and sustained.

These stages of developmental attention paralleled with findings of Gibson (1969), who suggested four dimensions to the normal development of attention:

Capture to Activity (Zero to Two Years). Initially, the infant's attention is involuntarily "captured" by stimuli, but gradually it becomes more voluntary.

Unsystematic to Systematic Search (Two to Three Years). Due to inefficient exploration strategies, the child tends to get stuck on one stimulus and finds it difficult to make transitions.

Broad to Selective Pickup of Information (Three to Five Years). The child is able to focus on a single aspect of a complex situation.

Ignoring Irrelevant Information (Five to Six Years). Gradually, the child is able to shut out unwanted information and concentrate on only the essential aspects of the information.

Children who are developing normally are believed to expand their attention spans as they relate and respond to information within their environment. The ability to demonstrate persistent concentration over a period of time is dependent upon intact cortical and subcortical brain function (Mirsky 1978). A hypothesized neurological component of attention deficits may be the factor that interacts with or impedes concentration and attention. If we understand normal levels of attention and observe it in same-sex classmates of the student, it may be possible to determine a child who presents symptoms suggestive of ADHD. The student with attention deficit disorder will perform differently during these developmental stages. This student will be observed to be more to the extreme and more suggestive of the symptoms of ADHD. For example, an observer would watch a group of same-sex classmates as they work on a puzzle. This would be followed by observing the student with attention challenges in the same situation. The observation data would be collected and symptoms recorded. (For example, "Jason seems to attend to the puzzle 15% of the time, while the other same-age boys in his class attended an average of 70% during the same observation session.") Direct observation of the child in a staged activity time is one way to provide data on current behavior. This observation data gives us a range in which the child with attentional concerns is either below or strongly above the normal expected levels of attention. If the student with difficulty is above or below age-expected norms, we are identifying the possible symptoms of the disorder.

Diagnosis of Attention Deficit Disorder: Early Childhood

Within early childhood development, the diagnostic process typically begins when the preschool teacher observes a child's problem with learning, behavior, or underachievement, or when the parents alert the teacher to their concerns. The diagnosis of attention deficit disorder is most appropriately made at the early ages by a multidisciplinary team, with both the teacher and parents being critical parts of the team. The purpose of gathering information from a combination of measures and observations in a multidisciplinary format is to provide an interpretive profile of the child which incorporates various areas of development and psychological functioning. During the information-gathering process, priority is given to observation checklist and parent checklist data.

Observation

Observation, usually by the classroom teacher or school psychologist, is the initial tool in effectively documenting the child's level of attention and distractibility. Observation should occur in a variety of settings, including:

- During solitary, parallel, and group play
- At home with parents, siblings, and other significant people
- In new environments, such as therapy session or the doctor's office

The goals of the observation are:

- To describe the child's general behavior and how it relates to the criteria established in the *DSM-IV*
- To observe skills in a variety of areas to determine what delays are present
- To note any atypical behaviors that warrant more formal testing, such as weak visual-motor skills noted as the child copies his or her name or a design
- To describe interactions with peers in a combination of activities that demonstrate social loneliness, social anxiety, and other responses

These observations form the core for basic information required to confirm the diagnosis and begin to understand the child's actions. Once the observational data has been collected, the teacher then compiles the data and presents a written referral to the appropriate party—perhaps a supervisor or the child's study team or diagnostic team—who then initiates the assessment process. The assessment should include:

Clinical history
Parent interviews
Teacher interviews and observation
Parent rating scales
Teacher rating scales
Psychometric evaluations
Test coordination motor ability
Cognitive achievement testing (if appropriate)
Language assessment (if appropriate)
Physical examination, including screen of ears and eyes

Diagnosis

In assessing preschoolers, special emphasis must be placed on the severity and frequency of disruptive behavior rather than on its presence or absence (Campbell 1990). In making a diagnosis of attention deficit disorder, the following components are to be examined:

- *DSM-IV* diagnostic criteria
- Interview and observation information from parents and teachers, especially inferences of the sources of difficulty. Parents who are unaware of developmental norms (for example, parents who have no other children) tend to overreport problems with their children due to unrealistic expectations, thereby engendering additional conflict. Conversely, some parents may be overly lenient and, thus, fail to notice potential problems (Landau, et al. 1991).
- Scores obtained on the rating scales and checklists
- Difficulty in areas requiring attention; documenting of objective measures
- Available information from combined data indicating significant discrepancies among the areas considered

In making a diagnosis with input from the school team, Goldstein and Goldstein (1990) suggest that problems of attention disorder behavior should cause the child difficulty in at least 50% of school/interaction situations. The assessment tools listed below are commonly used as parts of a multidisciplinary evaluation covering a diversity of areas. This list is provided as an overview and should not be considered an endorsement of the relative merit of these tools. Evaluations should always be administered by developmental professionals with appropriate training. This list of instruments includes interview questionnaires that document a child's medical and developmental history. Questionnaire interview formats are nonthreatening methods of obtaining information and are easy to complete. Additional instruments include assessments of vigilance, attention levels, and psychoeducational batteries. Checklists to be completed by both parents and teachers are a part of the assessment and provide valuable daily documentation of behavioral components. It is important to know which checklists have been normed for preschoolers and which ones may be developmentally inappropriate for this age group. The assessment of preschool youngsters introduces some unique problems that require an often different approach to evaluation. Neuropsychological disorders frequently are displayed on the variable measures as diffused rather than discrete conditions, which complicates questions related to diagnosis, individual program planning, and prognosis. Neurological impairment, even when documented by hard medical evidence, is highly variable in its expression from one age to another (Hartlage and Telzrow 1986).

Although there are obvious assessment limitations, the importance of early identification of developmental challenges will be critical. Research has indicated that intervention in the early childhood years results in greater success for these individuals.

Assessment Tools

Interview

ANSER System: Aggregate Neurobehavioral Student Health and Education Review (Levine 1981). Contains Parent Evaluation, Teacher Evaluation, and Self-Evaluation forms

Childhood history form for attention disorders (Goldstein and Goldstein 1990)

Interview with child

Teacher Rating Scales

ADD-H Comprehensive Teachers Rating Scale (ACTeRS) (Ullman, Sleator, and Sprague 1985)

Teacher Report Form (Achenbach and Edelbrock 1986)

Conners Teacher Rating Scales (Conners 1989)

Academic Performance Rating Scale (DuPaul, Rapport, and Perriello 1990)

School Situations Questionnaire (Barkley 1997)

The Yale Children's Inventory (Shaywitz 1987)

Parent Rating Scales

ADD-H Comprehensive Parent Rating Scale (Ullman, Sleator, and Sprague 1997)

Conners Parent Rating Scale—Revised (Conners 1997)

McCarney Home Rating Scales (1989)

Visual Motor Memory Integration

The Developmental Test of Visual Motor Integration—Revised (Beery and Buktenica 1997)

Visual-Motor Gestalt Test (Bender 1989)

Impulse Control

Matching Familiar Figures Test (Kagan 1964)

Wechsler Preschool and Primary Scale of Intelligence. (Wechsler 1967)

Wechsler Intelligence Scale for Children—3d ed. (WISC-III). Mazes subtest. (Wechsler 1991)

Wechsler Preschool and Primary Scale of Intelligence—Revised. (WPPSI-R). Mazes subtest. (Wechsler 1991)

Cognitive Ability

Bayley Scales of Infant Development. 2d ed. (Bayley 1993)

The Kaufman Assessment Battery for Children (KABC) (Kaufman and Kaufman 1983)

Woodcock-Johnson Psychoeducational Battery—Revised. Early Developmental Scale (Woodcock and Johnson 1989)

Diagnostic Inventory of Early Development—Revised (Brigance 1991)

Self-care skills

Basic Language Skills

Receptive-Expressive Emergent Language Scale—Revised (REEL-R) (Bzoch and League 1978)

Peabody Picture Vocabulary Test—Revised (PPVT-R3) (Dunn and Dunn 1997)

Token Test for Children (DiSimoni 1975)

Test of Auditory Comprehension of Language—Revised (TACL-R) (Carrow 1990)

Key Factors

Many other assessments are unsuitable for a preschool child either because they are not normed for this age group or because they require skills that are beyond the child's developmental level. When evaluating young children, observing their approach to the task is often more informative than are standardized test scores. Note the following behaviors as you test, and use these questions as a guideline to help you chart atypical activity. Base your recording of responses on the information given at the beginning of this chapter (see Normal Development of Attention Control, pages 15–17) and on prior experience working with children the same age *without* suspected attentional challenges. Record any responses that identify atypical behaviors in the child's movement, as well as communication skills and socialization skills that might warrant further exploration. In particular, the preschoolers with ADHD should demonstrate greater emotional response in their reactions to a task or activity. They are less mature in the self-regulation of emotion because of their deficiencies in behavioral inhibition. Thus you will see more overt gestures and reactions (for example, face making or verbal comments: "Oh, no!"; "What?"; "Ugh!"). You should also notice more challenges with making a choice or selecting one item. Last, they will impulsively scan, point, and tap at the materials, often manipulating the clinician's materials themselves.

Record your responses to these questions:

1. Does the child impulsively answer questions (or select the answer in forced-choice format) without appearing to think about alternatives?

2. Does the child fidget even when appearing interested in a task?

3. Does the child's conversation appear random or sound like a "free flight of ideas"?

4. Does the child continually look away from tasks in response to noise and other visual distractions?

5. Does the child frequently comment on extraneous noises or objects in the room that are unrelated to the task at hand?

6. Does the child frequently ask questions such as, "When will the game be over?" "What's next?" or "What other games do you have?"

Other methods of informal observation also are helpful. For example, children with attention deficit often have more than the usual amount of challenge with remembering sequential activities. They will have difficulty remembering the names of colors or the correct order of the alphabet. They may be able to sing the alphabet song, but will not be able to identify the letters when asked to repeat them or point to them. Although they have learned their own names, at times they may write them incorrectly or leave out letters. This suggests weaker memory for attention to detail and concerns with impulsive response. They often think ahead about what is coming and do not complete the activity they are working on immediately.

Cognitive tests are important, but place a greater allowance on observation, parent-report data, and teachers' check scales. An expert in developmentally appropriate behavior is an important member of the early childhood team when reviewing diagnostic testing material.

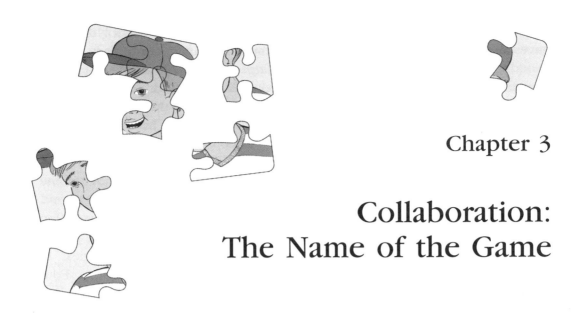

Chapter 3

Collaboration:
The Name of the Game

Teacher Assistance Team, Multidisciplinary Team, Individual Assessment Team, Child Study Team—no matter what the terminology, the purpose is that a team of caring professionals is discussing and using their expertise to best evaluate and provide support for a child. Children with attention deficit, like any other children, benefit from observation and evaluation of a multidisciplinary team. The team approach in managing attention deficit brings together individuals from different disciplines who contribute their expertise, share in decision making, and provide strategies for intervention. The multidisciplinary team process is not new, and for a child with documented special needs, it is a requirement of the public law (PL 101-476, the Individuals with Disabilities Education Act, called IDEA). The value of a team or collaborative approach for the child with attention deficit is that it offers a well-defined reservoir of data on the child and provides interpretations from varied professional perspectives.

Team members serving preschool children should be trained in all aspects of child development. The needs of an individual child will influence the membership of the team. As a particular component of the child's strengths and weaknesses emerges during diagnostic testing, professionals from other disciplines may be invited to join the team to better meet the child's needs. The collaborative team approach is applicable in a medical setting or an educational, mental health, or other facility. In all situations, parents are integral members of the team.

Parents

As soon as the child enters any type of formalized learning experience, be it day care, preschool, or kindergarten, the parent of that child begins to be part of an educational process that will continue for more than eighteen years. The majority of parents will never experience being a member of a multidisciplinary team focusing specifically on their child. For parents of a child with special needs, however, it will soon become a matter of fact.

routines, and generation of consistent behavioral consequences (Searight, Nahlik, and Campbell 1995). According to Goldstein and Goldstein (1990): "The physician's role includes directing the search for remedial medical causes of ADHD, participating in the multidisciplinary diagnostic evaluation, and, when medication is indicated, supervising the medication intervention programs" (52).

In addition, part of the physician's role can be to provide checklists (rating scales) to parents, educators, school nurse, and other significant people in the child's life to assist in documenting behaviors. One instrument designed to facilitate history taking is *The ANSER System* Parent Questionnaire (Levine 1981). This questionnaire carefully documents areas of concern observed by parents and educators. When this information has been collected under the direction of a physician, a treatment program can be designed that involves various members of the team.

School Nurse

The school nurse is a valuable member of the team process. Training in recognizing normal growth and development, observing and recording behaviors, and communicating with physicians and families are experiences that make the school nurse an important part of a collaborative effort. The nurse also can offer current information to parents regarding the effectiveness of treatments, can identify local physicians with particular expertise in attention deficit, and can provide help in forming support groups.

The nurse can facilitate the information-gathering phase by helping teachers and parents complete the questions and checklists; observing the child in school, home, and play environments; calculating results of checklists and rating scales; and formulating patterns of similar observations. Once the assessment data has been recorded and the diagnosis established, the nurse's role shifts to collaboration with school personnel, the family, and the physician. If intervention includes a pharmacological component, the nurse communicates with the physician throughout the therapeutic trial period, during which the individual child's correct dosage is established. The nurse will need to gather observation and data as before-and-after documentation of behaviors and to observe the child for side effects. It is important that the nurse regularly monitor the child on medication using the following measures: height, weight, blood pressure, objective observations of a rating scale, teacher's weekly progress reports, and parent and physician conferences.

Once a physician has established the dosage, the preceding measures can be taken less frequently, based on input from physician and parents. The nurse then will set up an effective, organized method of dispensing the medication. Effective management includes finding positive ways to ensure that children remember to take their medication on schedule without drawing negative attention to the matter. Suggested means of doing this include:

1. Offer behavioral incentives (for example, stickers on a chart, points, or tokens for children who need positive reinforcement).

2. Keep lunchroom tickets or passes in the nurse's office, where children can take their medication before lunch and then proceed to the lunchroom.

3. Offer a place in the office where the child can take medication in privacy. The child may want to talk about the medication and other aspects of the disorder and treatment. The nurse can offer direct comment or precise responses to the child's questions.

4. Provide some books dealing with medication issues available for children. (See page 166 for suggestions.)

5. At the end of the day, offer peanut butter or cheese and crackers or other snacks for children whose appetites are suppressed by the medication.

6. Keep a confidential record of the type of medication taken, the dosage, and times taken.

Educational Specialist/Special Education Resource Teacher

The educational specialist, academic therapist, or special educator is responsible for evaluating the child's achievement and skills and for individualizing instructional programs for a child's needs. These specialists may be part of a team in school, a clinic, or a private practice. They function primarily to help the child within the academic environment.

The educational specialist plays an important role in determining how well the child with attention deficit responds to group instruction, and in providing information to the team regarding the child's academic performance. Efforts to mainstream children with special needs require that the special educator offer information to the regular educator regarding the child's strengths and weaknesses. The specialist can support the regular-education teacher by offering strategies for managing the child's behavior and suggesting instructional activities to maximize the child's potential.

The education specialist, the classroom teacher, parents, and therapists work together using compensatory strategies to help the child. All bring their areas of expertise to the cooperative effort of helping the child succeed. For example, the educational specialist knows what the child needs in order to learn how to write; the teacher is adept at using this information to procure the materials and activities that the student needs; and the occupational therapist is skilled at looking at the underlying visual motor skills needed for these tasks.

Psychologist

The school or clinical psychologist is responsible for giving and interpreting assessments that measure the child's general intelligence. These assessments include tests of attention, vigilance, and behavior patterns. The psychologist can compare the child's ability of achievement data gathered by the educational specialist to determine whether the child is eligible for any special education programming. The testing procedure can provide valuable information for understanding how the child focuses with mild frustration and assess to what degree the child is ready for a school-like environment. The school psychologist also can help to identify whether a 504 Plan (see pages 35–36) is appropriate for the child's educational accommodations. The psychologist addresses concerns regarding the student's strengths and weaknesses in academic areas as well as the child's emotional and behavioral status. Using data collected, the psychologist can offer interpretations of what the child might experience in different learning conditions. More important in the evaluation is the psychologist's observation about the child's accommodations to the structure, ability to follow directions, impulsivity, and perception of time.

Hartlage and Telzrow (1986) state that the major key in direct assessment of preschoolers is *flexibility*. Using that watchword, they feel they have not encountered an "untestable preschool child." The two psychologists share that if the child they are testing refuses a task, they immediately introduce a new one or, on occasion, move to chat with the parent and attempt the task again when the child's curiosity has been aroused. At times they employ concrete rewards, but have found this necessary with only a small number of children. They caution that the school psychologist should expect certain behaviors when assessing preschool children; and almost always in their experience, a failure to obtain some response from the child can be attributed directly to the examiner and not to the youngster.

The following are areas of cognitive functioning that a school psychologist or clinical psychologist may observe in recognizing differences between attention deficit students and their typical counterparts.

1. Students with attention deficits often display difficulties on tasks that require complex problem-solving strategies and organizational skills (Barkley 1990; Tant and Douglas 1982; DuPaul and Stoner 1994).

2. Students with attention deficit often have more difficulty relative to normal peers on tests of executive function. Strategies that children with ADHD employ on these tasks are inefficient, frequently impulsive, and poorly organized (Zentall and Kruczek 1988).

The school psychologist can collect, review, and examine the behavioral frequencies and observations, much in the role of the case manager. Although each of the aforementioned techniques is somewhat limited in preschool observation, when used in a multimodality assessment package, a system of checks and balances develops, such that the drawbacks of any single measure are balanced by data obtained through other means (Barkley 1988).

Speech-Language Pathologist

The initial assessment information may indicate a need for speech and language evaluation. Studies of the attention deficit-hyperactivity population suggest that a higher than average percentage of preschoolers with attention deficit also have speech and language problems (Baker and Cantwell 1987: Love and Thompson 1988). Specifically, 10% to 54% of children with ADHD may exhibit expressive language problems, relative to 2% to 25% of the normal population (Barkley, DuPaul, and McMurray 1991). George DuPaul and Gary Stoner make reference, in their book *ADHD in the Schools* (1994), to the research of Hamlett, Pellegrini, and Conners (1987), stating that children with ADHD evidence a high rate of disfluent (for example, misarticulations) and/or disorganized speech on tasks that require verbal explanation (for example, responding to reading comprehension questions). Zentall (1985a) also notes this pattern of less organized speech leading to a diminished influence of self-directed speech in controlling one's own behavior. Barkley and Mash (1996) further comment that the "impairment in reconstitution will be most evident in everyday fluency when the person with ADHD is required by a task or situation to assemble rapidly, accurately, and efficiently the parts of speech into messages (sentences) so as to accomplish the goal or requirements of the task" (74). The authors admit that the amount of evidence for a deficiency in verbal fluency is limited; but what exists, they believe, is highly consistent with this prediction of an impairment in verbal motor output.

Children who have ADD together with language problems exhibit certain characteristics that will alert an adult—in many cases, a parent—to the problem. Other difficulties are far more subtle and may be recognized only through in-depth evaluation.

These children may exhibit characteristic difficulties with communicative control. They appear unable to predict the consequences of their words and say inappropriate things at the wrong time. They often fail to recognize conversational cues, and their narrative discourse is disorganized. They have trouble taking the perspective of the listener in order to determine what communications will please, what will offend, and what will engender conflict (Levine 1987b). Thus, the behavior of children with ADHD often elicits controlling and negative communication from others, thereby reducing the help these children receive in learning to regulate their own behavior (Berk and Winsler 1995).

Listening skills evade these youngsters. They do not attend to relevant stimuli, and their lack of selective attention contributes to poor listening habits. They switch topics abruptly and lose eye contact. They are unable to use covert speech to monitor their impulsivity. Thus, they appear to act thoughtlessly and be unable to direct their planning internally. They will express tangential, unconnected thoughts, and often they fail to adapt their behavior to varying contexts.

Recent studies have focused on the relationship between parent-child interaction and children's use of private speech. Private speech is often described as verbal monitoring of one's self, a form of self-regulation. One parent told me, "I always know where Mike is in the house. I just listen, and I can hear him talking to himself as he plays."

Studies conclude that hyperactive children use more overt, task-relevant private speech while working on tasks than do same-age peers (Berk and Potts 1991; Berk and Landau 1993, Winsler 1994). These studies also noted that the self-speech of ADHD children often contained more irrelevant and off-task comments. When compared to the speech of children without behavior problems, the speech patterns of ADHD children appeared to be less related to their on-task performance and on-task attention. Once an adult began to use scaffolding (modeling) techniques to guide the child to understand how to use private speech, the child began to demonstrate a better task performance. After scaffolding, the child would use private speech in a more internal fashion as a tool of focus and attention. This research suggests that one way the speech pathologist might benefit the ADHD child would be by providing such scaffolding techniques, thereby helping the child to use private speech to generate efficient problem-solving strategies.

Many tests are available to evaluate the language skills of children. The skilled practitioner knows which tests are acceptable for individual cases. Some of the more commonly used language instruments are listed below. Measures that tend to be particularly sensitive to ADHD characteristics include tests of listening skills, repeating an auditory sequence of digits (auditory memory), imitating sentences, repeating an auditory sequence of words, and recognizing and using appropriate sentence structure (syntax).

Common Language Assessments

Receptive-Expressive Emergent Language Scale—Revised (REEL–R) (Bzoch and League 1978)

Preschool Language Scale—3 (PLS–3) (Zimmerman, Steiner, and Pond 1992)

Peabody Picture Vocabulary Test—Revised (PPVT–R3) (Dunn and Dunn 1997)

Test of Auditory Comprehension of Language—Revised (TACL–R) (Carrow 1990)

Test of Early Language Development (Hiresko, Reid, and Hammill 1981)

Token Test for Children (DiSimoni 1975)

Detroit Tests of Learning Aptitude. 2d ed. (Subtest of auditory attention span; also, Subtest of visual attention span for objects) (Hammill 1985)

Occupational Therapist

Occupational therapists use activity in adapted surroundings to facilitate the student's independent function in school and to minimize the effect of the disabling condition on the student's ability to participate in the educational process (American Occupational Therapy Association 1989). As a member of the multidisciplinary team, the school or clinic-based occupational therapist identifies the fine motor problems of the child with ADHD and makes and carries out recommendations for remediation (see table 3, page 33). The occupational therapist can help the teacher to form realistic expectations of the child's functioning in the classroom. For example, the teacher's expectations may be too high or too low regarding the child's ability to complete written assignments, to sit at a chair or desk for a certain length of time, to sit in a chair without squirming or falling, or to play appropriately at recess with peers.

The occupational therapist can ensure that the student maintains an effective posture for learning—sitting erect in a correctly sized table and chair with books and learning materials placed to facilitate visual tracking of the text. The occupational therapist also will ensure that the child's eye-hand coordination is adequate for copying from the chalkboard, and will develop interventions or compensatory strategies for children who have difficulty with visual-motor memory integration. This therapist serves as a resource for adapting and modifying the physical environment of the classroom to meet the child's specific needs (Royeen and Marsh 1988).

Typical reasons why a child with attention deficit may be referred for occupational therapy include:

1. Difficulty with visual-motor integration. Occupational therapy programs for the preschool student with visual-motor integration difficulties may include pre-writing activities, fine motor tasks, visual tracking, or sensory motor/sensory integration activities.

2. Difficulty tuning out excessive stimuli in the classroom. For the child with difficulty processing external stimuli, a program of activities that relax or inhibit the nervous system may help the child achieve a calm, alert state to enhance learning. This may help the student respond to high levels of stimulation in the classroom without losing control (Oetter 1986). The program may include tactile activities, deep-pressure activities, and a slow, rhythmic rocking or balancing. Other methods for relaxation in the classroom include changes in the environment, such as playing music, reading to the students, and using imagery.

3. Difficulty with motor coordination. Children who are impulsive may appear confused and clumsy. This may or may not be due to an actual deficit of motor coordination. It is critical, therefore, that a child who has been referred for motor coordination weaknesses be observed and considered carefully to determine the source of

the problem. There is a fine line between children who are awkward because they are not paying attention and children who have an actual deficit in motor planning.

Attention deficit disorder and sensory integration disorders have some common characteristics. For example, pre-term infants who are identified as having sensory processing deficits are characterized as being unusually restless and disorganized (Cermak 1988). Other commonalities include delay or disorder in the development of antigravity responses and unusual patterns of response related to reticular activating system function (Oetter 1986). Research, however, suggests that training isolated motor and visual motor skills is insufficient to benefit a learner with attentional problems (Kavale and Mattson 1983; Lerner 1988). In their book, *Attention Deficit Disorder and Learning Disabilities* (1993), Ingersoll and Goldstein note that there are significant discrepancies between the theory of control of sensory integration and attention deficit. Their research suggests that there is no reason to indicate that the vestibular system is primarily involved in regulating attention. They also believe that the notion that reading disorders stem from faulty eye movements or problems with visual perception has been examined with no significant research. They note, "There is no consistent evidence from well-controlled studies that supports integrative training as a treatment for children with attentional problems" (190).

A study conducted at the University of Toronto by Tom Humphries, Ph.D., compared sensory integration with a perceptual motor program. At the end of the study, children in both the control group and children with attentional concerns showed some improvement in motor skills, but there was absolutely no improvement in visual perception, handwriting readiness, copying ability, self-concept, or cognitive inattentional skills.

The term *sensory integration* was coined by Dr. Jean Ayres, an occupational therapist. She used this term to explain the brain's ability to organize stimuli and recognize information coming through all the senses. Many reports on sensory integration have been published since Dr. Ayres described her approach (Ayres 1979), but to date not one single study has met truly rigorous standards of acceptability. See table 3 for suggestions for managing problems commonly observed in children with ADHD, both in terms of intervention commonly conducted by an occupation therapist and general principles that can be well applied in other educational settings.

TABLE 3
Collaboration of occupational therapy

If the child has difficulty with:	Try this in OT:	Try this in other settings:
Staying on task	Present activities that involve strong muscle contraction.	Offer variety, brevity, and structure.
Becoming overexcited	Provide games with a definite start-and-stop action.	Slow down verbal directions and movements.
Tuning out	Use visual and auditory cues to help the child stay on task (for example, jump, tap, turn, shout, clap).	Provide order. Help the child see the sequential order in activities rather than just the whole activity.
	Playground activities include climbing and walking.	Use visual and auditory cues (tapping, focus words such as, "Eyes here," and moving around the room).
Sitting or standing still, tipping chair backward, bumping into objects, restlessness	Use exercises that involve balance, lying on one's stomach or back, or up-and-down movements, such as push-ups and chin-ups. Place class work on a slant board. Playground activities include swinging, sliding, and climbing.	Allow opportunities for movement in the room. Permit the child to work in alternative positions, such as kneeling or standing. Provide the child with two chairs in class; when restless, the child may move to the other chair. Break work into shorter segments. Reinforce the child for each step accomplished.

See figure 1 (page 34) for an example of an Individualized Education Program (IEP) for occupational therapy for Bart, a six-year-old boy diagnosed with a learning disability and attention deficit/hyperactivity disorder. Bart has particular difficulty with visual-motor integration, balance, and laterality. Notice that this IEP targets skills that have implications for academic performance, and many of these goals can be implemented in the classroom after consultation with an occupational therapist.

FIGURE 1
Sample IEP for Occupational Therapy

Name: Bart

Annual Goal	Anticipated Mastery Date	Criterion for Acceptable Performance	Mastery Date
1. Improve balance/ equilibrium responses on gravitationally secure and insecure surfaces	1/15	Bart will maintain balance on a tilt board in a variety of developmental positions (sitting, kneeling, half-kneeling, and standing) 8 out of 10 times (80%).	
2. Improve bilateral motor skills via graded activities	1/15	2a. Bart will use one hand to hit a balloon volleyball with a paddle on the right or left side of his body, as directed, on 8 out of 10 attempts. 2b. Bart will complete chalkboard activities that require his hand to cross completely to the other side of his body, without switching hands, 7 out of 10 times with verbal and physical prompts.	
3. Improve visual tracking skills via graded activities from games with large movements to more refined activities associated with academic tasks	1/15	3a. Bart will successfully keep a balloon in the air during a volleyball game on 7 out of 10 attempts. 3b. Bart will hit a sponge ball with a plastic bat 6 out of 10 times.	
4. Improve visual-motor control via graded activities incorporating games and activities	1/15	4a. Bart will hit a target with a beanbag 7 out of 10 times. 4b. Bart will successfully complete activity cards 8 out of 10 times.	
1. Improve balance/ equilibrium responses	6/1	1. Bart will demonstrate a delay of less than 8 months in balance skills on the *Brunniski Test of Motor Proficiency.*	
2. Improve bilateral motor skills	6/1	2. Bart will complete activities using contra-lateral sides of the body on 8 out of 10 trials.	
3. Improve visual skills	6/1	3a. Bart will visually track across a workbook page, successfully finding all the *h*s 8 out of 10 times. 3b. Bart will successfully track across a written page from left to right with no more than 3 errors per line.	
4. Improve visual-motor control	6/1	4a. Bart will successfully copy a design 8 out of 10 times. 4b. Bart will successfully complete activity cards on 8 out of 10 trials.	

Developing an Individualized Education Program or 504 Accommodation Plan

Children with attention disorders may be eligible for services and support under varying laws for children with disabling conditions.

Two important federal regulations can be part of the service plan for a student with attention concerns. They are Public Law 101-476, the Individuals with Disabilities Education Act (called IDEA), and Section 504 of the Rehabilitation Act of 1973. Federal regulations mandate a written Individualized Education Program (IEP) for each area in which a child is deemed eligible to receive services. Depending on the degree of interdisciplinary collaboration in a particular setting, each professional might develop a separate IEP for the child, or a joint IEP might be developed. The IEP is developed when the child with ADD has been identified as having an additional disabling condition, such as a learning disability or significant language delay. The 504 plan is developed when we do not necessarily have additional documentation of another disability but are interested in assuring that the child with attention concerns will not fail in the learning environment. Rather, we provide a series of interventions that should accommodate for the child's present weaknesses in attention, impulsivity, and hyperactivity. Section 504 protects all students with disabilities, defined as those having any physical or mental impairment that substantially limits one or more major life activities, including learning.

For young children, the accommodations can include clustering activities into short chunks, eliminating distracters in the immediate play area, designing a structured environment in the classroom, and providing immediate reinforcement. It may specifically state a behavior plan for caregivers, teachers, and aides to follow when excessive impulsivity is observed. The value of such a formal document is that it encourages the team to put in writing specific strategies to implement for the individual child. In this way, it helps guarantee the child the right to a free and appropriate education based on individual needs.

The accommodation plan presents a simple, one-page document that presents the nature of the concern and the basis for the determination of the disability. It then describes how the disability affects a major life activity, and designs some reasonable accommodations within the classroom. All team members give their suggestions. When the plan is finalized, it is signed and placed in the child's cumulative file. See figure 2 (page 36) for a sample of the Student Accommodation Plan used by the Arizona Department of Education.

FIGURE 2
Sample student accommodation plan*

Student Accommodation Plan

Name_____

Date of birth_____ Date of meeting_____

School_____ Grade_____

1. Describe the nature of the concern.

_____

_____

_____

2. Describe the basis for the determination of disability (if any).

_____

_____

_____

3. Describe how the disability affects a major life activity.

_____

_____

_____

4. Describe the reasonable accommodations that are necessary.

_____

_____

_____

Review/Reassessment date_____ (Must be completed)

Participants (Name and Title)

_____   _____

_____   _____

_____   _____

_____   _____

_____   _____

cc: Student's Cumulative File
Attachment: Information Regarding Section 504 of the Rehabilitation Act of 1973.

*Reproduced with permission of the Arizona Department of Education, 1993.

Providing Structure for the Child: Three to Six Years

1. Define a space where the child can work. Use carpet squares, mats, small rugs with borders, tape on the floor, and plastic hoops to define where the child may sit or start an activity.

2. Use timers to increase tolerance for structured activities and to allow an appropriate amount of time to complete an activity. The timer also serves to prepare the child for transition. ("You have two more turns on the trampoline, and then it is time for the balance beam. One. . . Two. . . ." The timer rings.)

3. Place small stop signs randomly around the room. Hang a paper traffic light in the center of the room. Remind the children to "Stop and check your speed." Teach the children to stop and look at the sign or light when they become overexcited. ("Stop and look at the light, Danielle. What does that yellow light tell you? What is your speed? Is it fast or slow?")

4. Minimize distracting noises in your area.

5. Offer calming music as a subtle background change. Good choices are environmental sounds, classical, New Wave, or flute music.

6. Add soft furniture in your work area—pillows, beanbag chairs, mats, wedges, cushions.

7. With an overactive, easily excitable child, present activities that are slow and regular. Offer visual and auditory soft cues and pleasant olfactory stimulation.

8. For inattentive children, present activities that are quick and slightly irregular, with strong visual and auditory cues. Use bright colors and strong odors.

9. Tape record a child counting slowly to as high as the child can. Play this tape when you need a rhythmic beat for an activity.

10. Use memory techniques to help the child recall information. Employ songs, patterns, rhymes, and color associations.

11. Encourage the child to listen to you by giving clear instructions and by directing the child to listen carefully. Pause between each step of the direction. ("Eyes forward. Now listen to me. These three pictures tell a story. One. . . two. . . three.")

12. Provide continual reinforcement and encouragement for each task the child accomplishes or attempts to accomplish. ("You know how to write all the letters in your name"; "Look, class. Tom knows the right way to get on a trampoline.")

13. Help the child to slowly wind down from active or stimulating times. Play a relaxing tape five minutes before the end of the activity to slow the pace and signal the end of the class.

14. Use colored chalk or colored markers to highlight information on a chalkboard or easel. Focus the child's attention by drawing a box around information, using arrows, and underlining.

Transition

At times, related specialists or therapists are working with the child outside the regular classroom. Students with attentional concerns often have difficulty with transition when leaving one activity or area and going to another. Certain activities can encourage transition to a special resource room or therapy sight and minimize difficulties:

1. Make a bright sign labeled "SUPER KID" (see the reproducible pattern). Attach it to a 12-inch loop of string. On the days when a child is scheduled for therapy, hang the loop by the daily calendar. Place small SUPER KID stickers on the child's desk or cubby or where the child's coat hangs. When the children enter the room, say to them, "Today is Super Kid day. Your teacher will have this sign hanging in the room. When it is time for you to come to therapy, this SUPER KID sign will be on your desk. That will mean that it's your turn to come to therapy."

2. Hang a large sheet of chart paper or newsprint just inside the door of the therapy room. Place a box of crayons or markers in front of it. Label the sheet, "Autographs, please." Ask the child to choose a marker of a favorite color or a color that matches an item of the child's clothing. Ask the child to sign in when entering your room.

3. Use masking tape to outline a path from the door to a chair or desk where the child is to work. Ask the child to walk along the tape to the work area. Change the pattern of the tape every two days.

   - Cut short pieces of tape, two inches in length. Make a broken line leading to the work area. The child tiptoes to the work area, stepping from strip to strip.
   - Roll one long strip of tape from the door to the chair. The child walks on the tape as if it were a balance beam.
   - Make a zigzag pattern for the child to follow.
   - Make a winding pattern, with the tape circling the table before leading to the chair.
   - Make a spiral path leading to the work area.

4. Keep a large plastic jar by the door. Next to it, place a basket of plastic counters shaped like teddy bears or other characters. Entering the room, the child puts a counter in the jar. Exiting, the child takes the counter out of the jar. This activity provides cues for starting and finishing a session.

5. Use a variety of reinforcers to encourage active participation—press-on stickers, points accumulated toward a prize, or primary reinforcers such as animal-shaped crackers or cereal pieces.

Pattern for "Super Kid" Cutout

39

Activities to Enhance Listening

1. Use visual and auditory cues to enhance the children's listening. Each week, post a new sign that focuses on attention and listening.

2. Glue animal faces or characters' heads to the ends of tongue depressors. Keep these puppets available during a lesson. When you notice a child not listening or "tuning out," hold up a puppet rather than verbally cuing the child. This offers a subtle cue for attention and listening.

3. Bring a small suitcase and three clothing items, such as pants, shirt, and a tie. Tell the children, "I have to pack this bag for my friend, Paul. First the pants, then the shirt, then the tie." As you talk, pack the items; then close the suitcase. Ask the children to remember what you put in first, second, and last. Ask a child to pack the suitcase the same way you did. Provide other materials for different suitcase activities. For example:

    Packing for a baseball player: Ball, mitt, baseball cap

    Packing for a baby: Blanket, baby clothes, baby's hat

4. Introduce a small, stuffed mouse. Tell the children, "This mouse's name is Whispers because it has to whisper so the cat won't hear." Say to one child, "I'm going to let you hold Whispers while I tell this story. Every time I say the word *cat,* hide Whispers in your hand." Ask the children to whisper anything they may want to say during the story. Tell a brief story that contains the word *cat* several times. If a child becomes too excited, switch roles and have the child tell the story while you hide the mouse.

    Follow the activity with Whispers by introducing a finger-play exercise and a follow-the-leader game.

    > Jack-in-the-box sits so still.
    > (*Children enclose thumbs in their fists*)
    > Won't you come out? Yes, I will! (*Thumbs pop out*)
    >
    > How quiet can you be?
    > Can you be as quiet as I can?
    > (*Tiptoe around a carpet square; children follow*)
    > Can you be as quiet as a bunny?
    > (*Teacher and children hop like bunnies*)
    > Can you be as quiet as a baby asleep?
    > (*Teacher and children pretend to be asleep*)
    > (And so on)

5. Make a puppet by drawing a face on the palm of a large, white garden glove. Sew a red button on the index finger of the glove. When you are doing specific activities that require listening, place the glove on your hand. When a child appears to be tuning out or is distracted, point to the activity with the pointer finger. Make the puppet "dance" at the top of the child's papers or on the table in front of the child to redirect attention to task.

Patterns for Puppet Cutouts

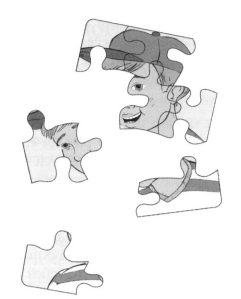

Chapter 4

The Merits of Early Identification

Although our knowledge and experience with infants with attention deficit disorder is limited, recently early intervention methodology and knowledge of clinical infant mental health have grown considerably. Early intervention in the late 1980s and into the 1990s expanded in growth and focus, and it is now holistic in nature with a systems theory base. As Zeanah and McDonough (1989) note, "The new studies focus on both family and child characteristics. These include family functioning, personal well-being and mental health of each family member, styles of parent-child intervention, and child behavior and development, with a particularly strong emphasis on social competence" (127).

Early identification of children who are at risk for ADHD benefits both the child and the child's teachers because it helps prevent the development of many further difficulties. Lerner (1988) points out that early intervention leads to a significant improvement in quality of life for these children and a substantial financial savings for society. Barkley's longitudinal study in 1981 suggested that 60% to 70% of children later diagnosed with ADHD had identifiable symptoms during their preschool years.

Of particular interest to early childhood educators is the increasing population of infants prenatally exposed to drugs or alcohol. These children show many characteristics similar to children diagnosed with attention deficit. They score in the low-average on standardized developmental assessments, show difficulty with social development regarding building and sustaining relationships, are easily distracted, need broad-planned transitions, and have difficulty with emotional development (Howard, et al. 1989; Viadero 1989). Newborns exposed to drugs in utero are not the rewarding, interacting, well-organized, competent infants that easily stimulate parental feelings of warmth and protection. On the contrary, interaction and self-regulation are usually poor, demanding that the environment provide external organization so that at least some limited interaction is possible. Nonlife-threatening essentials for the drug-exposed newborn your warm hands and fingertips over the child's forehead and eyes. Keep the child's head in midline by gently cupping the chin with one hand.

3. Guide the infant to suck on a thumb or pacifier to gain self-control through sucking.

4. Avoid dynamic, loud activity within the infant's or toddler's sight and hearing.

5. Feed the infant in a quiet, darkened room. A rocking chair provides soothing motion for feeding and quiet times. Use the same chair, type of bottle, and procedure consistently for feeding.

6. Be aware of physical distractions within the child's environment, and avoid sensory overstimulation. Sensory stimuli to avoid are a loud radio or television, a fan moving in front of a light source, a computer printer running, flashing lights, or defective fluorescent lighting.

7. Gradually provide the child with more opportunities to observe people or activities. If the child becomes stressed, swaddle it tightly and give gentle verbal reassurance along with soft strokes.

8. Avoid sudden changes in environmental conditions. For example, avoid taking the infant or toddler directly from air conditioning to hot air outside.

Guidelines for the Infant's Environment

1. Provide an airy and softly lighted room for the child. Have window coverings that can completely cover the windows when needed, to avoid any unusual or distracting light patterns.

2. Initially, place the infant in a bassinet or small basket. When the child is ready for a crib, fill half the crib with soft blankets so the child's movement is limited.

3. Avoid filling the crib with a variety of toys. Choose one soft toy to remain in the crib.

4. Some children are overstimulated by brightly decorated sheets that have busy patterns. Experiment with light pastel colors.

5. Use a sturdy infant or toddler seat. The child needs to feel secure and stable in any situation.

6. Gradually introduce a toy to attract the child's attention.

7. If the child loses interest in one object, do not introduce another one immediately. Rather, wait for a while, then slowly introduce a new object.

8. Alternate bright, shiny objects with others that have strong contrasts between light and dark.

9. Place small toys (a teething ring, one-inch cubes, a cup) within the child's reach on a brightly colored place mat that has a border.

10. To improve grasp, offer cereal pieces and other small, edible objects. Place them in small, brightly colored bowls.

11. Begin to offer a variety of patterns or textures for the child to explore. Place textures on the child's bedding. If the child withdraws or reacts negatively to a new pattern or texture, slowly withdraw it.

12. Stimulate laughing by light tickling.

13. When talking to the infant, hold the child upright at eye level so your face is clearly visible.

14. Hold the child close to you as you rock. Sing and hum gently. Use soothing, reassuring words at bath- and bedtime.

15. Use tepid water in the child's bath. Place a towel on the bottom of the tub to help control the child's movements. Blow bubbles for the child to observe and touch. Put squeaky toys in the tub. Use an oversized towel for drying, and hold the infant or child securely. Apply baby powder gently, rubbing slowly with a soft fingertip action.

16. Begin "patty-cake" and "peek-a-boo" games.

17. Give the child an opportunity to drop objects in containers and then spill them out.

18. Attract the child's attention by moving push-pull toys toward the child. Encourage visual tracking of objects.

19. Place an object within the child's field of vision. Let the child observe it. Slowly introduce a second object for the child to play with, and remove the first object. Then reintroduce the first toy while the child continues to play with the second.

20. Attract the child's attention with a variety of objects—small jingle bells, squeaky toys, mobiles, finger puppets, and similar objects. *Caution: Do not make sounds directly behind an infant's head, but rather to the side.*

21. Observe the child's reactions to auditory and visual stimuli. Record any signs of tension in the body, such as struggling to move away, flushing of the skin, or eye aversion. Share this information with the child's doctor.

Rock 'n' Roll

Goals

1. The child will follow an object.
2. When an object disappears, the child will refocus on the place it first appeared.

Materials

Brightly colored cylinder or toy on wheels
Small, solid-colored towel

Instructions

Place the child in an infant seat on a table or flat surface. Bunch up a towel on the table at the child's left side, and place a toy on the right. Attract the child's attention to the toy. Roll the toy across the table in front of the child to the towel. Observe whether the child follows the object to the towel and then looks back to where the toy started from.

Variations

"Walk" a small stuffed toy across the table to the towel.

Use a wind-up toy.

Hide-'n'-Seek

Goal   The child will find an object covered with a cloth.

Materials   Small, familiar object
2 solid-colored towels

Instructions   Seat the child in front of two towels placed 5 inches apart. Show the object to the child, then hide it under one towel. Encourage the child to find it.

Hide the object again under the same towel and encourage the child to seek it.

Then hide the object under the second towel to see whether the child can shift attention to a second location.

Hands-On Activities: One to Two Years

Controlling Inappropriate Motor Output

Hands-On Ball

Goal The child will control inappropriate motor output.

Materials Small, textured rubber balls (such as Koosh® balls) in a variety of sizes and colors

Instructions When the child is required to remain seated for a time (for example, in a car seat or while getting a haircut), provide a small, textured ball for restless hands to hold.

Color Alert!

Goals
1. The child will focus on a simple play activity.

2. The child will increase visual attention to task.

Materials
Bottom part of a sturdy shirt box
Brightly colored paper
Small blocks in solid colors

Instructions
Cover the inside of the box with the paper. Seat the child on the floor in front of the box. Arrange several small blocks in a tower inside the box. Place the remaining loose blocks in the box with the tower. Model building towers for the child.

Variation
Add other building materials—colored blocks, textured blocks, or blocks containing bells.

Hands-on Activities: Two to Three Years

Transition

Twinkle, Twinkle

Goal

The child will be prepared for changes through the use of rhymes.

Materials

Rhythm blocks or bells

Instructions

Prior to a change in activity (physical or visual), prepare the child for transition by introducing a soothing rhyme or rhythm. If you use certain rhythms or rhymes consistently, the child eventually will associate them with a change in activity. For example (to the tune of "*Twinkle, Twinkle Little Star*"):

> Blocks and toys must go away.
> Now it's time to end our play.
> To the bathroom we will go.
> You will be the first, I know.
> When the bell rings, it is time.
> No more toys now! Get in line.

Simple Steps to Matching

Goal From two or more objects, the child will select the one most similar to a model. (See Bailey and Wolery 1984.)

Materials 2 each of the following items: ball, shoe, spoon, toy car

Instructions Place one object on a table (for example, a ball). Seat the child at the table. Hold up an identical object, and instruct the child to find the match. ("Find the ball.") Give a variety of directions involving the ball. ("Give me the ball"; "Touch the ball"; "Look at the ball.") Present each item individually in the same manner. Then place two objects in front of the child and repeat the procedure. Gradually increase the number of items from which the child must choose.

You and Me and 1, 2, 3

Goals
1. The child will learn to play with others.
2. The child will perform a repetitive action with toys.

Materials
Small, brightly colored carpet square
Dishpan containing four familiar toys

Instructions
Place the carpet square across from you on the floor, and ask the child to sit on it. Place the dishpan between you. Pick up one toy and hand it to the child. Instruct the child to "Hide this toy behind you." Repeat with each toy in turn. Then ask the child to return the toys to the dishpan.

Variation
Give the child practice following verbal directions by giving a variety of instructions as the toys are returned to the dishpan. ("Put the red toy back in the pan"; "Use both hands to pick up two toys"; "Put the blue toy on top of the red toy in the pan.")

Chapter 5

Managing ADD: Three to Six Years

I am often asked, "What kind of teacher will be most successful with the child with attention concerns?" I believe it is the teacher who has strong affective skills; that is, one who uses the physical "look" or body language that carries meaning to the activity or verbal statement. Children with ADD will learn more successfully when the adult's body language quickly interprets meaning for them. Body language involves eye contact, body carriage, facial expression, gestures, and certainly physical proximity. Affective body language gives children the immediate feedback they need and communicates visually what the adult is expressing. Children with attention deficits will do better in a learning environment in which the adult has strong physical mannerisms that reinforce the child's behavioral limits. Strong facial gestures—a smile, a wink, "the look," a frown—and physical gestures—thumbs up, high five, putting a hand on one hip, standing up very straight—add to this visual message.

Younger children with attentional concerns often have difficulty making eye contact with the person to whom they are speaking. Because they are so easily distracted and stimulated by the environment, they are always looking at a variety of things or fingering or touching an item; thus, they find it difficult to look at one thing. Sometimes well-meaning adults will take the child's face in their hands and force the child to look at the adult. This is a negative technique and only creates friction with the child, who usually pulls away. A preferred style is to model appropriate eye contact. As the child's eyes move while talking, allow your eyes to follow the child's eyes. Provide positive verbal reinforcement every time you see the child making good eye contact. It also is helpful to stand in the general proximity of the student who looks around. Always give instruction to the eyes, not the side of the face or the back of the head.

Understanding Abilities

When we discuss young children with attention concerns, we tend to talk more about their *difficulties* than their *strengths*. We need to be aware that by knowing and focusing on attempts to improve the children's strengths, we can bolster their self-esteem and help them to see what they can do well.

65

TABLE 4
Typical strengths and weaknesses of children with ADD

Strength	*Weakness*
Verbal skills	Listening
Quick application of skills	Poor planning and follow-through
Visual big-picture skills	Visual detail
Long-term memory	Short-term memory
Intense emotions	Impulsivity
Enthusiasm, curiosity	Easy boredom
Activity movement	Impatience

In managing children with attention concerns, a teacher must take into consideration that although they can verbally express their needs, they often do not listen to what others are saying. They will tune out verbal detail. Thus, it is important to remember this thought:

The least effective way to correct a child with an attention disorder is by verbal correction alone. These children respond best to visual and verbal cues together.

Three Principles of Instruction

Three principles are critical when working with children who experience attention difficulties (Jones 1989a):

Brevity: Activities of short duration

Variety: Novelty or the slightest change in the activity to maintain continued interest

Structure: A consistent routine, enhanced by a highly organized format of activities

Research indicates that attention and concentration for these youngsters are greatest in short activities. Therefore, the use of *brevity*—frequent brief lessons, covering small chunks of information—will result in greater learning.

Because children with attentional difficulties tend to perform more poorly on the second presentation of a task, adding *variety* as the task is sustained will pique interest and maintain follow-through.

Novelty will heighten stimulation and alertness; yet within this, a *structured form* or organized plan lends stability and security. Clearly state rules, expectations, and consequences. Specific daily schedules that include well-planned experiences with smooth, well-defined transitions from one task to another are the keys for managing these children.

Variations of these principles will be helpful for all students and will enhance the learning environment. When planning the activities for the day, ask yourself, "Am I including brevity, variety, and structure in my plan for this child?" How well these three principles will improve the potential of students with attention deficits, only time and continued research will tell.

Management Suggestions:
Three to Six Years

Review this checklist when encountering problematic situations in the early childhood environment.

If the child has difficulty:

—Starting an Activity

- Give a signal to begin working.
- Present work in small amounts.
- Explain the purpose of the assignment.
- Provide immediate feedback and encouragement.
- Use a digital timer, and have the child estimate how long the assignment will take.
- Place a colored dot next to each activity. Tell the child to bring you the dot when the activity is done. Returned dots earn privileges.

—Staying on Task

- Remove all distractions from the work area.
- Place the child next to a peer who can help immediately.
- Employ color to highlight repetitive rote.
- Increase the frequency of reinforcement.
- Encourage eye contact.
- Build success into the task.
- Offer variety in tasks.
- Place work on a brightly colored paper, tray, or place mat.

—Staying Seated

- Make sure the child understands your expectations.
- Give a reward any time the child is sitting.
- Take a photo of the child sitting appropriately. When necessary, cue the child by pointing to the photo.
- Move the child's seat or desk away from distractions and nearer to the center of the room, across from you.

(continued)

—Following Directions

- Give short, concrete directions.
- Provide visual, auditory, and tactile examples.
- Repeat directions.
- Repeat directions in a different way.
- Have the child repeat and explain the instructions before beginning.
- Team the child with a peer who understands your directions.
- Ask the child to role-play what you asked the child to do.

—Working Independently

- Provide activities that are appropriate to the individual child's developmental level.
- Be certain the child can foresee an end to the task.
- Give brief, precise directions.
- Give frequent reinforcement. Praise the child in front of peers for concentrating.
- Alternate short, independent tasks with assisted tasks.
- Gradually require more independent work before giving help.

—Calling Out

- Reward the child immediately for listening.
- Reinforce peers who do not call out.
- Point to a cue posted on the wall to remind the child not to interrupt. (The cue could be a picture of a smile or just a colored symbol. Explain the cue to the child privately before class.)
- Give the child an opportunity to be a leader.
- Provide small-group exercises in which the child has the opportunity to share.

(*continued*)

—Needing a Great Deal of Personal Attention

- Assign a peer or volunteer for support.
- Check with the child at the beginning of a lesson.
- When the child does something right, draw attention to it immediately.
- Give redirection when the child gets stuck on one activity or subject.

—Following Classroom Rules

- Post rules in the classroom where they can be reviewed daily. Illustrate the chart with photos of children in the class following the rules.
- Make the rules simple. State them in language children understand.
- Be consistent in your expectations and consequences for breaking the rules.
- Give each child a list of the rules, if needed. Set up a "contract" privately with the student, and help the student verbalize the rules. Use pictures or drawings for younger children.

—Listening

- Provide visual models for the child to follow.
- Have the child repeat instructions aloud.
- Have the child sit in the front of the room or close to where you teach.
- Have the child act out what he or she has heard.

—Remembering

- Use mnemonics to cue recall.
- Have the child repeat directions into a tape recorder, and play the tape for the child to hear.
- Use songs, poems, and chants to enhance recall.
- Review activities periodically.
- Color code significant details.

Sugerencias para el Manejo:
Tres a Seis Años de Edad

Si el niño tiene dificultad para:

—Iniciar alguna actividad

- De una señal que significa que es hora de comenzar a trabajar.
- Presente la tarea en trozos pequeñas.
- Explique el proposito de la tarea.
- Proporcione refuerzo y apoyo inmediato.
- Use un cronometro y haga que el niño calcule cuanto tiempo va a necesitar para completar la tarea.
- Peque una pequeña calcomania en forma de círculo junto a cada actividad. Pídale al niño que le traiga el circulo despues que él termine esa actividad. Para cada círculo devuelto se gana un privilegio.

—Mantener el interés

- Retire todas la distracciones del area de trabajo.
- Siente al niño junto a un compañero que le pueda ayudar inmediatamente.
- Use color para resaltar tareas rutinarias y repetitivas.
- Aumente el refuerzo.
- Fomente el contacto visual.
- Incluya éxito en la tarea.
- Proporcione una diversidad de tareas.
- Coloque la tarea sobre un papel o charola de color brillante.

—Quedarse sentado

- Asegurese que el niño entiende lo que usted espera de él.
- Dele un premio cuando esté sentado.
- Tome una foto del niño sentado apropiadamente. Cuando sea necesario, señale la foto para recordar al niño que debe estar sentado.
- Aleje el asiento o esritorio del niño de cualquier distracción y póngalo más hacia el centro del salón, en frente de usted.

(continua)

—Seguir instrucciones

- De instrucciones cortas y concretas.
- Proporcione ejemplos visuales, auditivos y tactiles.
- Repita las instrucciones.
- Repita las instrucciones de manera distinta.
- Haga que el niño le repita y explique las instrucciones antes de empezar la tarea.
- Junte al niño con un compañero que sí entiende las instrucciones.
- Pídale al niño que actue lo que usted le acaba de decir.

—Trabajar independientemente

- Presente actividades que son apropiadas para el nivel de desarollo del niño.
- Asegurese que el niño sepa que la tarea terminará.
- De instrucciones breves y precisas.
- De refuerzo frecuentemente. Frente a los compañeros, alabe al niño por poner atención.
- Cambie de tareas breves e independientes a tareas acompañadas.
- Gradualmente, haga que el niño trabaje más independientemente antes de pedir ayuda.

—Quedarse callado

- Premie al niño inmediatamente cuando escucha callado.
- Refuerze a los compañeros que no interrumpen la clase.
- Indique una señal sobre la pared que le recuerda al niño que no debe interrumpir. (Por ejemplo, la señal puede ser un dibujo de una sonrisa or simplemente un símbolo en color. Explíquele el significado de la señal al niño en privado, antes de la clase.).
- Dele al niño la oportunidad de ser el líder.
- Organize actividades que se pueden hacer en grupos pequeños para que el niño tenga la oportunidad de compartir en la actividad.

(*continua*)

—Requerir mucha atención

- Asigne a un compañero o a un voluntario para que le ayuden a usted.
- Chequee con el niño antes que usted empieze una lección.
- Cuando el niño hace algo bien, llámele la atención inmediatamente.
- Redirija la atención del niño cuando el o ella se queda fijado sobre un solo tema o actividad.

—Sequir las reglas del salón de clases

- Fija la lista de las reglas en un lugar en el salón donde se puedan revisar por diario. Agregue dibujos o fotos a la lista que muestran niños portandose bien en el salón.
- Haga reglamentos sencillos. Use palabras que los niños pueden entender.
- Sea constante en cuanto a lo que se espera del niño y cuáles son las consecuencias de no seguir los reglamentos.
- Dele a cada niño su propia lista de los reglamentos, si es necesario. Redacte (en privado, junto con el niño) un "contrato" y ayude al estudiante a repetir las reglas en voz alta. Para niños chicos, use dibujos.

—Escuchar

- Proporcione ejemplos visuales.
- Haga que el niño le repita las instrucciones en voz alta.
- Pídale al niño que se siente al frente del salón o cerca de usted.
- Dígale al niño que "actue" lo que acaba de escuchar.

—Recordar

- Use la mnemonica.
- Haga que el niño grabe las instrucciones en una grabadora, y luego tóquelas.
- Use canciones, poemas y cantos para ayudar la memoria.
- Revise las actividades periodicamente.
- Use colores para resaltar detalles importantes.

Guidelines for Intervention

The Learning Environment

1. Although individual children vary in their ability to selectively ignore stimuli, many teachers have found that classrooms free from extraneous auditory and visual stimuli are most suitable (Telzrow and Speer 1986a). The complete removal of distractions is *not* warranted, however. Reducing the degree of stimulation aids in focusing attention, but removing all distractions does not help these children significantly. In fact, some evidence suggests that such efforts are counterproductive (Douglas and Peters 1979). Children with ADD appear to be internally distracted and can lose concentration even in the most sterile environments.

2. Maintain an orderly room. Establish a system for organizing materials, such as coding by color or number. These techniques help the teacher to efficiently manage the materials that the children will be using.

3. Brief lessons result in greater learning. Chunk learning tasks into small, well-defined steps, and present the information sequentially.

4. Minimize the time spent waiting, and maximize "on-task" time.

5. Offer frequent visual, verbal, and physical feedback. Remember that verbal cues are not the most salient means of reinforcing children with attention problems.

6. As you speak, face the children directly. Present information in an area in which you can physically and visually reinforce concentration.

7. Modeling or demonstrating activities allows children to learn visually and to improve their recall.

8. Color code relevant features to capture the children's interest. (*Caution: Do not allow color to become an added distraction.*)

9. Employ devices to enhance short-term memory. (See pages 120–125 for suggestions.)

10. Move around the room during a lesson, gently tapping children on the arm and maintaining eye contact with them.

11. Maximize eye contact. Reward eye contact and attention immediately.

12. State directions in a brief, positive manner. Reinforce what will be accomplished.

13. Avoid giving directions in groups. When children are asked to gather in a close group, they are more interested in their personal space being invaded than in the directions or lesson being presented (Cook, Tessier, and Armbruster 1987).

14. Encourage children to take turns giving directions to each other. When they become distracted or bored, introduce the activity in a different way.

15. Provide activities that are developmentally appropriate and offer success. Select interesting and meaningful tasks.

16. Ignore minor fidgeting, wiggling, tapping, and similar movements. Provide opportunities for purposeful movement. For example, if John continually taps his fingers on the table, you might respond by handing him a toy cash register and asking, "John, can you make this cash register work?"

The Playroom

Arrange the playroom space to offer opportunities to work individually, in small groups, or in large groups. Provide a variety of well-defined action stations.

1. Encourage active children to move and explore, but also promote planning skills by providing structured areas.

2. Store toys in boxes on shelves. Glue pictures on the boxes to label the contents.

3. Group similar materials in a marked box to provide a classification tool for children and to encourage the development of association skills.

4. Place materials that the children are allowed to access within reach to encourage exploratory play.

5. Place extraneous materials out of sight.

6. Provide ample activity centers and duplicates of popular toys and materials so children don't have to wait to participate.

Childproofing the Environment

The impulsive behaviors of children with attention deficits make them prime candidates for accidents. Offer a "child-safe" environment that is secure and predictable.

1. Check the working environment, and remove all potentially dangerous objects.

2. Cover all electric sockets, and secure loose wires to the floor.

3. Remove tools, sharp objects, and any faulty equipment from the area.

4. Select classroom materials for children's use based on their durability. (Impact-resistant plastic toys are better choices than delicate toys with many intricate pieces.)

A Special Place for Special Things

Children who have difficulty with organization and planning often forget where materials are kept in the room, and they require order in their environments.

1. Make a place for each child's belongings. Label the space with the child's name or an identifying symbol chosen by the child. Let the child keep this same place throughout the school year.

2. Provide marked boxes for storing a variety of things, from "take-home" papers to lunch boxes and boots.

Preferential Seating

Children who do not spontaneously turn and look at the teacher for directions will benefit from careful placement within the room.

1. During large-group activities such as circle time, seating children in a semicircle is most efficient. Seat the children with ADD directly across from you, where you can easily maintain eye contact.

2. For small-group activities, place chairs or carpet squares in a semicircle. Guide the children with ADD to places in the center, directly across from you.

3. Place good role models on either side of each student with ADD.

4. Reward children for going to their seats and for paying attention.

5. Avoid giving directions or demonstrations when children are behind you or to your side. Children will respond best when they can look directly at your face.

6. Some children will feel more comfortable having two assigned chairs in the room. This way, they can move from one chair to the other when they feel restless.

7. Some children are less restless when they sit backward in the chair (that is, astride the chair with the back between their legs). This prevents them from tipping or rocking the chair and gives a large base of support.

8. Place tape on the floor, and write each child's name on the tape. When activities are on the floor, the children look for their names on the tape.

Independent Work Time

Children with ADD need to be encouraged to work independently for short periods of time. Self-checking and self-pacing activities promote inner control.

1. Let the children's activity levels and attention spans dictate the activities you introduce and how long you expect the children to stay with the tasks.

2. Follow the children's leads, and allow them some choice in selecting materials.

3. Model and teach strategies for following classroom rules for turn taking, passing materials, and sharing.

4. Place materials a child has selected directly in front of the child on a brightly colored sheet of paper, in a tray, or on a section of plastic or linoleum tile. This will help to define the work area for the child.

5. When children are engaged in a hands-on activity on the floor, define their work areas by providing movable carpet squares, flat baskets, trays, or plastic hoops.

6. Place tape marks on the floor to designate starting points for games, where to sit for circle time, where to form lines, and other activities.

7. Offer children privacy boards (small cardboard shields) to isolate activities on a large work table.

8. Allow the children to use a screened area within the room as a private work area, when necessary. For this strategy to be effective, be sure the children perceive the private area as a choice or alternative, rather than as a punishment.

9. Encourage children to sit in beanbag chairs when they look at books. The chairs cushion movement and provide security in one spot.

10. Encourage children to lie on their stomachs during independent writing or coloring. This reduces free or random movement of arms and provides a sense of security.

Daily Routine

Children with ADD function better in a classroom that has a consistent routine. Arrange the schedule so that there is a predictable format for the day, even though the specific exercises within each time slot may vary from day to day.

1. Plan highly routine schedules with a regular time for daily experiences such as snack time, calendar time, and nap time.

2. Present activities that are appropriate to the children's developmental levels and within the range of their abilities.

3. Each day, post a visually animated schedule, and review it with the class for several minutes. Cross off each completed task.

4. Incorporate certain rituals for transition, such as a song to be sung during cleanup or a bell that signifies time to wash before a snack.

5. During particularly noisy times in the room, soft background music serves as a calming agent.

Transition

Unexpected changes in the daily plan or movement from an unstructured activity to a structured activity may cause significant behavioral problems in children with ADD, due to their tendency to easily become overaroused and their challenge in moving from one setting to another. Because transition activities make up 25% of a child's school day, planning for transition times is important. Time countdowns and advance warnings will help the children to anticipate change and respond more appropriately.

1. Employ auditory and visual cues to signal changes in the daily routine.

2. Present code words, songs, or visuals to help the children anticipate and make transitions. Cues for lining up and moving, both within and outside the classroom, promote attentive behavior.

3. Schedule time for the transition to occur. As you close one activity, review several interesting or motivating aspects of what is coming next.

4. Use cues to signal that the children have just a few minutes to complete their work. Verbally and visually prepare them for the next experience.

5. Give specific directions regarding how to move to the next activity.

6. In front of classmates, positively reinforce and recognize individual children's abilities to move from one activity to the other. Reward students for making orderly and smooth transitions.

Color Association

The effectiveness of using color to draw attention to relevant discriminative stimuli has been well documented (Zentall and Kruczek 1988). You can use color to highlight important features within a task.

1. Add color accents to key features of repetitive tasks that children with ADD often find boring and unmotivating.

2. Avoid adding color simply to increase the attractiveness of a task; this may create an added distraction, especially for young, overactive children. If the task has not been overlearned, their performance may deteriorate (Zentall and Kruczek 1988).

3. For older children who are learning letter sounds, highlight any difficult sounds. For example, a flash card for a child having problems with "silent-e" words might look like this:

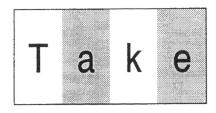

4. Color code large areas in the room to help with the day's planning. Hang a brightly colored triangle over the kitchen area, another colored triangle over the block area, and so on. When discussing the daily plan, mention the activity and its color as a specific memory cue.

5. Color code specific smaller areas in the room. For example, designate a red box for storing morning kindergarten library books, and a blue box for storing afternoon kindergarten library books.

Increasing Children's Attention

The ability to focus attention and concentrate on the task at hand is paramount in learning. Children who have difficulty attending will benefit from exercises to enhance their concentration.

1. Present objects with clear and obvious dimensions—large blocks, simple shapes, cutout alphabet letters.

2. When first presenting an activity, use a limited variety of materials (for example, only large, red circles).

3. Make available only the materials that are necessary. Place materials in front of each child on a tray, colored paper, or a place mat.

4. Use puppets and visual cues (a magic wand, a pointing finger, and so on) to draw students' attention.

5. Employ "key words" to improve listening. Call out the child's name; or use words such as "Focus!"; "One, two, three!"; "Look!"; "Listen!"; "Eyes on me!"

6. Present rules and directions in the form of chants or songs to give a rhythm pattern to the information.

7. When teaching the entire class, have everyone repeat directions orally.

8. Speak with a slow, even tempo. Present information in short chunks with pauses between them. Eliminate lengthy descriptions.

9. Ask the child to repeat directions to you or to a classmate. Provide a tape recorder so children can randomly repeat directions and then listen to their own voices.

10. If children are engaged in negative activity, redirect their attention to a new stimulus. For example:

    Jason: Maggie, I want gum.
    Maggie: Jason, look at the wheels on this truck!
             One is not turning.
    Jason: Maggie, I want gum.
    Maggie: Look, Jason. This wheel stays still when I push.
    Jason: Gum! Gum! Gum!
    Maggie: Jason, I need you to push the truck.
             Can you fix the wheel?

With this question, Maggie puts the truck into Jason's hand. Jason looks at the truck and begins to examine it (Jones 1989b).

Enhancing Children's Self-Control

One of the components of attention deficit disorder is impulsiveness. Most children with this condition have poor self-control. Parents and teachers report that these children are unable to contain motor and verbal outbursts. They have difficulty waiting their turn or waiting for complete instructions. Impulsiveness negatively influences their interactions with their peers and could have an impact on their social development. Experiences in stopping and starting an action on a signal, and in self-pacing or regulating their responses, will help these children to develop self-control. This type of practice can be initiated in the preschool classroom as well as the therapy environment.

1. Provide activities that have a definite beginning and ending. Announce this by song, puppet, key words, or a visual (for example, by placing a green transparency on the overhead).

2. Offer practice in starting and stopping an action on a signal (for example, pouring liquid into a cup).

3. Use visual and tactile cues to help children mark the passage of time (for example, each child places a peanut in a large jar every day before a designated field trip to the zoo).

Time-Out

An out-of-control, overstimulated child may need to leave the environment temporarily. Time-out is just one tool in an effective behavior management program. It works best with a variety of incentives, behavioral reinforcers, and modeling opportunities. Its effectiveness is diminished when it is used continually, because it reduces the child's opportunity to interact with others. A more successful intervention is to restructure the learning environment in a way that provides successful experiences for the challenging child.

1. Designate a chair to the side of the class as a time-out place. Have the child face the class to realize what is being missed.

2. Barkley (1987) recommends a time-out period of one minute for each year of a child's life (that is, time out for a four-year-old child is four minutes). For more active children, two minutes may be the limit.

3. Set a timer for the determined amount of time.

4. At the end of the time-out period, ask the child three questions. As you speak, use a visual clue of three raised fingers.
   - What happened?
   - What should you have done?
   - What will you do next time?

5. Avoid long rhetoric. Focus on only the three questions. Use them to show the child how to use verbal coaching to gain self-control.

6. Guide the child in finding ways to handle anger and frustration. ("When you get angry at Sarah, come and talk to me about it.") Display a poster of different facial expressions. Discuss openly how we look when we are angry, happy, sad. Point to the expression, and ask, "Is that how you feel today?"

Strategies for Promoting Social Interaction

1. Children with ADD may lose their train of thought in the middle of telling you something and fail to complete the message. They may respond to this experience by muttering to themselves or saying, "Never mind." Respond by directing the child to "Tell me that again" and giving appropriate encouragement by putting your hand on the child's shoulder and smiling.

2. These children are easily distracted, and their verbal discourse may become confused and irrelevant. If this happens, ask questions to structure the child's narrative. Use a positive tone of voice when you ask, for example:

   - "What are we talking about?"
   - "What did we decide?"
   - "Did we already talk about that?"
   - "When did this happen?"
   - "What?"; "Where?"; "How?"

3. Give feedback when you observe appropriate social responses.

   - "I like the way you took your turn. Friends will want to play with you when you take turns like that."
   - "The way you just let me go ahead of you lets me know that friends will like to play with you."
   - "You know what to do to make friends happy. Friends like people who take turns like you do."

4. Set up activities in which the children can work together. Designate children to help each other with specific tasks.

   - "Molly and Ryan, let's see what you can do with the building blocks."
   - "Jason and Helen, would you pass the papers together? When you help each other, it makes the work easier."

   See *Let's Be Social,* a language-based social skills curriculum, for additional ideas (Social Integration Project 1989).

5. Teach the children how to play board games and activities that other children might enjoy playing with them. Model socially appropriate playing skills, and reinforce children for imitating these skills. ("I like the way you said, 'Your turn now.' Friends will like it when you talk like that.")

6. Have a special theme week during which each child can bring a favorite teddy bear to class. Each day, plan an activity in which the bears can model sharing, taking turns, and other social skills. Celebrate the last day with a bear party featuring bear-shaped cookies. Discuss good manners. Send each child home with a bear tag reading, "Bear with Me."

Activities to Enhance Thinking Skills

1. Choose a brightly colored hat that you identify as a "thinking cap." Ask questions that guide the children to problem solve and to begin thinking logically. Begin with very concrete and easy questions. As the children's skills increase, progress to more complex questions. This is an excellent transition activity for leading into a lesson or therapy session. Begin by saying to the children, "I have my thinking cap on. It's time for 'head work!' Put your thinking caps on, too. (*The children put on imaginary caps.*) Well done, thinkers! Here's our head work for today."

Sample Beginning Questions
Auditory Comprehension

> Show me your favorite color.
>
> How old are you?
>
> Put your hand on your head.
>
> Show me how to hop.
>
> Point to _____. (*Name a child in the room.*)

Word Finding/Verbal Fluency

> Name two animals.
>
> Name two kinds of food you like.
>
> Name two things we write with.
>
> Name two kinds of pets.
>
> Name two things we use on our hair.

Intermediate Questions
Auditory Comprehension

> How many noses do you have?
>
> How do you know when a dog is angry?
>
> Would you like to fly up to the moon?

Word Finding/Verbal Fluency

> Name all the people who help us.
>
> Name all the things we can eat for breakfast.
>
> Name all the sounds you hear at the zoo.

Basic Reasoning

> Do you feel happier when you lose a game or when you win?
>
> How many eggs could you hold in your hand at one time?
>
> You can drink water. What else can you do with it?
>
> Can you kick with your hands?

Advanced Questions

A boy and his mother were in a room. The boy said, "There's something burning on the stove." What would make him say this?

There are three children in a family: Jason, Jennifer, and Dan. How many brothers does Jennifer have?

What is the difference between a calendar and a clock?

Could you go places more easily with a broken leg or with a broken arm? Why?

Why might clothes that once fit you become too tight for you?

As Carmen and her mother were looking out the window, Carmen said, "See how hard the wind is blowing." How did Carmen know it was windy?

2. Hold up a large brown paper grocery bag. Ask the children, "What could we do with this bag?" At first, the children will give very conventional answers, such as, "Take the garbage out in it." Encourage them to begin thinking creatively. Give them suggestions. ("Could I put my foot in it? Could I tie the top to make a shoe?")

Next, hold up a small bag, such as a resealable plastic bag, and ask, "How could we use this bag?"

Then remove the bags and show a piece of colored yarn. Continue to question the children, and encourage them to brainstorm.

3. Take instant photographs of children doing different activities, such as sitting at a table putting together a puzzle. Take a picture of one child's face and another picture showing the same child doing the activity. Show the picture of the child's face, and ask, "What do you think Doug is doing in this picture?" Encourage the children to interpret from the facial expression what might be happening. Then show the complete picture. Ask, "Did you know that Doug was working on a puzzle? How do we look when we're working hard on something? What made you think Doug was working on something difficult?"

4. As you watch the children throughout the day, photograph them modeling a variety of facial expressions—sad, happy, sleepy, excited, looking thoughtful. Display the pictures, and ask the children to discuss how they think the child in each picture feels.

5. Play the game called, "If You Were." Ask the children to picture themselves in a certain situation. Then give them a choice of equipment (or present two strategies for handling the situation), and ask them to decide which they would prefer.

If you were climbing a mountain, which would you rather use—a pick or a pair of hiking boots?

If you were in a snowstorm, which would you rather have—heavy mittens or snowshoes?

If you were caught in the rain, which would you rather have—an umbrella or a raincoat?

6. Cut out magazine pictures of various actions (for example, a car in a service station being repaired, a woman making breakfast, a man loading clothes into the washer). Show each picture. Ask four questions about each picture, and discuss the replies.

What is the problem? (or, What is happening?)

What should (I, you, they . . .) do?

What do you think will happen?

Did that take care of the problem (or job)?

Use these four questions in the context of classroom activities. Remind children to ask themselves these questions when they have difficulty recalling information or solving a problem. Teach them to say the questions aloud and then to themselves. Ask them to close their eyes, think over the questions, and then answer them aloud.

7. Use private-talk techniques to help children become more involved in what is happening in the classroom. Have them practice private talk, first aloud and then silently. Teach children how to talk their way through an activity. ("What does the teacher want me to do? Oh yes, I'm supposed to copy the picture. Okay, first I draw a line here. . . .")

Teach children to give themselves positive messages when they complete a task. ("How about that! I did it!") Children with ADD use more private talk or self-instruction talk than their peers. It is often a way for them to focus. Help them to use it in a positive manner.

Resources: Management

There are several effective management resources that can provide additional guidance to teachers, caregivers, and parents. These include:

Barkley, R. *Defiant Children*. New York: Guilford Press, 1987.

Jones, C. *Young and Active: Strategies for Elementary Students with ADHD*. San Antonio: Communication Skill Builders, 1997. (Video)

Moorman, C., and N. Moorman-Weber. *Teacher Talk*. Saginaw, MI: My Institute of Personal Power, 1989. (Phone: 517-791-3553)

Parker, H. *Behavior Management at Home: A Token Economy Program for Children and Teens*. Plantation, FL: ADD Warehouse, 1995. (Phone: 1-800-233-9273)

Phelan, T. 1995. *1-2-3 Magic: Effective Discipline for Children 2 to 12*. Glen Ellyn, IL: Child Management.

Keeping Order

Goals 1. The child will use association clues.
2. The child will improve recall.

Materials Containers, such as:
  Egg cartons
  Trays
  Plastic bottles
  2-inch-deep boxes
  Milk crates
  Silverware storage trays

Labels
Pictures indicating categories of box contents
Glue

Instructions Use a variety of containers and boxes for storing classroom materials. Keep similar materials together in one box to help the children learn classification skills. Clearly label each box on the outside with a picture of its contents. Use silverware trays or egg cartons for organizing materials that the child is using on a table.

Name Tag Central

Goals   1. The child will learn organizational skills.
2. The child will stay with one activity for a longer period.
3. The child will learn to make choices.

Materials   Colored construction paper
Marking pens
Scissors
Masking tape
16-inch lengths of yarn
Boxes for storing tags

Instructions   Design signs for the activity centers in the room, and post them in the centers. For example, in the kitchen center, place a tag shaped like a kitchen utensil; in the art area, use a tag shaped like a paintbrush; and in the water corner, post a tag shaped like a bucket.

Make smaller tags that match the activity center tags, and attach a loop of yarn to each one so the children can wear them like necklaces. Place a box for storing the tags in each activity center. When children want to play in an activity center, ask each child to take a tag from the box and wear it. Teach the children to return the tags to the box before leaving that center and going to another one. Circulate through the room. Ask the children which center they're in, and talk to them about what they are doing during their play time. This strategy helps impulsive children to see a beginning and an end to each experience.

My Choice

Goals

1. The child will learn to plan an activity.
2. The child will select materials for play in an orderly manner.

Materials

Pictures of activities and materials in the room
Scissors
Tagboard
Glue
Hole punch
Book rings or ribbons

Instructions

Mount each picture on a piece of tagboard. (You may want to laminate the pictures with clear plastic for durability.) Punch a hole at the top of each card. Place these activity cards in front of the child. Encourage the child to choose two activities to do. Place the two activity cards on a ring to attach to the child's belt or on a ribbon to wear around the neck. Tell the child, "Here is your plan. You may play with the activities you chose. When you are finished, you may come back and choose others."

Let's Go Walking

Goals   1. The child will follow sequential directions.
2. The child will maintain attention on a task.

Materials   Large picture cards that illustrate three-step sequences

Instructions   Place the pictures in random order on the chalk tray or on the floor. Have each child take a picture and line it up in the correct order. To reinforce the sequence, encourage the children to stand in front of their pictures or stand on them in stocking feet. Ask the children questions about why they put the pictures in that order. ("You put toothpaste on the toothbrush before you brushed your teeth. Why?")

Bucket Brigade

Goals
1. The child will learn to work independently.
2. The child will learn to wait for help.

Materials
Empty cottage cheese or yogurt containers (one for each child)
Colored polystyrene peanuts or small cubes

Instructions
Observe the child during independent work time. Record how many times the child calls for assistance during a series of brief time periods. Average the numbers from all your observations. Decide how many peanuts or cubes to give the child based on the average number of requests (for example, five requests in five minutes). Explain that you are proud of the child for learning to work independently. Present the bucket with the five cubes in it. Tell the child, "Every time you call me during free time, I will take a cube. If there are any cubes left at the end of five minutes, you will get a sticker." Gradually increase the length of time and reduce the number of cubes. Praise the child for working independently during free time.

Snowman Stack

Goals

1. The child will recognize shapes.
2. The child will improve attention for visual clues.
3. The child will use a memory strategy to help with recall.

Materials

6 white circles in ascending size
Large felt-tip pen
Paper hat for snowman
Envelope for storage
Red construction paper (4-inch square) or index card
Green construction paper (4-inch square) or index card
Tray

Instructions

Number the circles from 1 to 6, with 1 being the largest and 6 being the smallest. Begin by using only three of the circles. Place the circles in a tray in front of the child. Explain that the child is going to build a snowman. Ask the child to describe step by step how to build it. (Be sure the child can count from 1 to 3.) Place the green card on the tray directly in front of the child, and place the red card at the top of the tray to indicate where to start and stop. Have the child put the largest snowball on top of the green card, then place the remaining snowballs in order of descending size to reach the red card. Place a hat on the snowman. When the child can consistently stack the three circles in order, introduce all six circles.

What Happened First?

Goals   1. The child will learn to sequence activities.
2. The child will attend to details.
3. The child will follow directions.

Materials   Picture sequence cards
Green construction paper (4-inch square) or index card
Red construction paper (4-inch square) or index card
Number cards

Instructions   Place the green card on the table to the child's left, and place the red card to the child's right. Explain that green means to go or start, and red means to stop. Encourage the child to place the sequence cards in chronological order between the green and red cards. Then give the number cards to the child. Encourage the child to place the numbers in order above or below the sequence cards.

What's First?

Goals   1. The child will follow a routine.
             2. The child will work on specific skills during independent time.

Materials   Name tags and holders (one set for each child)
             Materials that lend themselves to IEP goals; for example:
                      Puzzles
                      Lacing boards
                      Matching and sorting games
                      Nesting cups

Instructions At the beginning of the day, set up the children's name tags at the table. Select a goal area from each child's IEP. Locate an appropriate activity to reinforce that skill, and place it by the child's name tag. As the children enter the room at the beginning of the day, guide them to their name tags and have them take their activities to their individual stations. After they have completed their tasks, they may have free time until all the students have arrived. This strategy helps to organize a room in which children arrive at different times. Each child always knows what to expect first. For each skill, record the child's progress for IEP records.

Classroom Helpers

Goals

1. The child will learn classroom responsibilities from role models.
2. The child will be given cues to fulfill classroom responsibilities.
3. The child will improve auditory and visual recall.

Materials

Bulletin board or wall chart
Instant camera and film

Instructions

Designate one child each day to be "Direction Helper." When you give a direction, the helper will stand next to you, model or act out your instructions, and repeat them. Throughout the activity, the helper will be available for children who need to hear the instructions again.

Take instant photos of children modeling appropriate classroom behaviors and performing various classroom responsibilities (such as napkin passer or line leader). Post the photos around the room or on a bulletin board or wall chart. Use them to cue the children to desired behaviors. For example, at circle time, ask, "How many people are sitting like Jeffrey is in the picture?"

Variation

If the directions have multiple steps, give the helper cards that illustrate your instructions step by step.

Starting the Day with a Song

Goals   1. The child will understand times of the day.
                   2. The child will be given a sequential list of daily activities.
                   3. The child will follow a routine.

Materials   None

Instructions   During morning circle, sing songs and recite chants that name the days of the week and the activities that took place on those days.

Songs   (To the tune of *"The Farmer in the Dell"*)
                   On Monday we had music.
                   On Monday we had music.
                   Heigh-ho-the-derry-oh.
                   On Monday we had music.

                   On Tuesday we had library.
                   (And so on)

                   (To the tune of *"She'll Be Comin' 'Round the Mountain"*)
                   If you're glad today is Monday, clap your hands.
                   If you're glad today is Monday, clap your hands.
                   If you're glad today is Monday, if you're glad today is Monday,
                   If you're glad today is Monday, clap your hands.

                   If you're glad today is Tuesday, stomp your feet.
                   (And so on)

**Weekday   1-2-3-4-5, Go!
Chant**
                   Monday, you are number one.
                   I hope this week is lots of fun.

                   Tuesday, Tuesday, look at you!
                   I guess you know you're number two.

                   Wednesday, Wednesday, number 3.
                   Two days left to go, I see!

                   Thursday, you are number 4.
                   Now there's only one day more.

                   Friday's here! The week's gone by.
                   One to five, just see time fly!

                   1-2-3-4-5, Go!

Poem   Good morning, good morning,
                   Good morning to you!
                   We're glad you are here!
                   Our day should be grand.
                   I need you to help,
                   So please lend a hand.
                   From stories to music, to snack and to art,
                   We have work to be done, so let's all play a part.

How I Start My Day

Goals

1. The child will use a memory technique to recall a sequence.
2. The child will attend to oral directions.
3. The child will control impulsiveness.

Materials

Action pictures (or instant-camera photos) of children:
>Washing face
>Washing chin
>Washing ears
>Brushing teeth
>Brushing hair

Cardboard squares
Glue
Tongue depressors
Stapler

Instructions

If possible, take photographs of children in the class modeling the activities listed above. Mount the pictures on cardboard squares, and staple each one to a tongue depressor. Display the pictures with the children, and discuss each picture. Give one picture to each child. Recite the following poem, and have children hold up their pictures when their activities are mentioned in the poem.

>I wash my face, I wash my chin,
>I wash my ears outside and in.
>I brush my teeth, I brush my hair.
>I'm ready now. Let's go somewhere!

Transition

Moving Right Along

Goals
1. The child will move from one exercise to another smoothly.
2. The child will remember the progression of activities in a day.

Materials None

Instructions Plan the day to begin with unfocused activities, and move gradually to more focused ones; for example, recess (unstructured); song time (slightly structured, allowing for freedom of movement); group listening activity such as storytelling (more structured); and, finally, independent work at a table (structured).

The following chants are helpful in recall and in easing transition:

> *Putting away toys:*
> Time to put the toys away.
> Put them away for another day!

> *Moving to a chair:*
> Touch your nose, then touch your hair.
> Hurry now! Go find your chair.
>
> Find a chair, find a chair.
> Find a chair, and sit right there.
>
> This is my place. Find your chair.
> Sitting places are everywhere.

> *Taking turns:*
> Taking turns is fun to do.
> One for me, and one for you.

> *Lining up:*
> There's the bell! Hear teacher call,
> "Line-up time for one and all."

> *Snack time:*
> Pass the napkin, pass the snack
> When you're finished, pat your back.

> *Returning to the classroom:*
> Chairs, chairs, all in a row,
> Help us know just where to go.

Transition

Count Down!

Goals   1. The child will move purposefully to the next activity.
2. The child will be aware of the passage of time and the time remaining for an activity.

Materials   Green, yellow, and red table-tennis balls
Marking pen
Large clear jar

Instructions   Number the green ball 1, the yellow ball 2, and the red ball 3. Place them in a large clear jar. When children are working on an activity with time constraints, display the jar containing the balls. As you walk around the room, observe how much time is left in the lesson. Remove one ball from the jar at regular intervals, beginning with ball number 1. When only one ball is left in the jar, announce that time is almost over. When time is up, remove the jar as you discuss the upcoming activity. The colors of the balls add another ordering cue for children, as they proceed from green (GO) to yellow (SLOW) to red (STOP).

Transition

Leaving One Activity to Start Another

Goals

1. The child's frustration at leaving a task and starting a new one will be reduced.
2. The child will be positively directed to the next activity.

Materials

Puppet
Timer
Tape player and audiotape of music

Instructions

Incorporate consistent activities into the daily routine to signal when the class will move from one activity to another. Allow time for transition. Before the change, let the children know what is coming next. ("Put your crayons away carefully. Well done, class! Hands on your desks. We will be going out for recess, and we can bring several balls with us. Listen for your name.") Reward students for making orderly transitions.

Variations

Use a puppet to introduce story time or other special experiences. Have the puppet announce what's coming.

Use songs to move from one activity to the next.
> Time to put the toys away,
> Toys away, toys away.
> Time to put the toys away,
> And go on with our day.

Throughout the day, alert the children before you move to another activity. ("We have five minutes until story time. I've set the timer for three minutes, so I can remind you to pick up your toys.")

Play a specific musical piece on the tape recorder to signal transition. For example, play "Zippidy-Do-Dah" when it is time for recess.

Transition

Snip It!

Goals
1. The child's frustration will be reduced at leaving a task and starting a new one.
2. The child will be positively directed to the next activity.

Materials
Colored construction paper
Scissors
Glue
Classroom daily calendar

Instructions
Make a paper chain, with one link corresponding to each activity on the daily calendar. Choose a particular color to represent each activity (for example, circle time = blue; story time = green; snack time = yellow). Hang the paper chain by the classroom daily calendar. Choose a child to cut off the corresponding link as you finish each activity. (When hanging the chain, remember that the children will need to cut from the bottom up.)

Transition

Getting Ready

Goals
1. The child will be positively directed to the next activity.
2. The child will anticipate an activity over an extended time.

Materials
Balloons
String or ribbons
Calendar

Instructions
During circle time, discuss with the children an upcoming special event, such as a proposed field trip in three days. Review the rules for field trips, and role play events that may happen on the trip. Blow up three balloons, and tie one above each intervening day on the calendar. Each day, choose a child to pop one balloon.

Variation
When a child repeatedly asks, "Is this the day of our trip? Is it?" point to the balloons and ask, "Did you check the balloons? How many are left? What does that mean?" Reinforce the children for checking the balloons.

Follow Me

Goals
1. The child will learn to take turns.
2. The child will follow verbal cues.
3. The child will practice age-appropriate social interactions.
4. The child will improve auditory memory.

Materials None

Instructions Stand in front of the children, and tell them to do as you do. Hop on two feet. Wait for the children's response, then imitate it. Use a gesture (extend your hand, bow, or point to a child) to signal whose turn is next. Then let a child take the lead while you and the other children imitate what that child does. Continue to follow the children's lead, doing and saying things that are equal in length to what they do.

My Turn

Goals
1. The child will learn to take turns.
2. The child will be guided to control impulsive actions.
3. The child will practice age-appropriate social interactions.
4. The child will improve auditory memory.

Materials
Orange construction-paper circles
Marking pens

Instructions
Choose a game or activity that can be played in a small group. Write each child's name on an orange circle. Place the circles name-side down on a table. Ask one child to choose a circle and read the name on it. That child will go first. Then the next child chooses a circle to determine who goes second. Number each circle above the name as it is chosen. Continue until all names have been chosen. Place the circles clockwise around the table in the order chosen, and have the children sit in front of their circles. Play the game or activity. When a child moves out of turn, tap the number on the child's circle as a cue.

What Will You Do Next?

Goals
1. The child will learn to plan more than one activity at a time.
2. The child will learn organization skills.

Materials
Drawing paper
Marking pens

Instructions
Give the children sheets of paper on which they will draw their plans for independent work time. Ask each child to describe the plan. Then ask, "This is your first plan. What will you do after that?"

Variation
At the end of work time, ask children to act out the order in which they performed their tasks, using their plans to help them remember.

Cooperation

Partners

Goals

1. The child will learn to work with other children.
2. The child will follow step-by-step directions.

Materials

Trays (one for each child)
Box of hands-on materials, including:

> Stamp and envelope
> Ring and ring box
> Doll's sock and shoe
> Plastic glasses and case

6 pairs of cotton socks, adult size, each pair a different color

Instructions

Have the children choose partners. The partners group the materials in the box into pairs of associated objects. Question the students about why they put each pair of objects together. Then have them place each pair of objects in a matching pair of socks and return them to the box. Pass out pairs of socks to the children and have them describe the contents.

Free Play

Interest Centers

The use of centers within the classroom provides a variety of exciting experiences for preschoolers. In addition to more traditional centers, the following will stimulate play:

Art Center
Various art media—colored pens, large chunks of chalk, scrap paper, different colors of foil, ribbon, glue, craft sticks, watercolor sets, tagboard, construction paper, large sheets of newsprint

Business Center
Various office supplies—calculator, adding machine, cash register, receipt pad, stamp pad, pens, box of play money, spectacles, telephone, computer paper

Hospital Center
Play medical equipment—stethoscope, hospital paper masks and hair caps, adhesive bandages, clipboard, tongue depressors, knee pads, finger brace

Space Center
Walkie-talkies, globe, space helmets, instrument panels made from boxes, resealable plastic bags (for specimens), rocks

Computer Center
Computer, printer, computer paper, software, rewards (stickers and certificates)

Language Center
Tape recorder, typewriter, paper, pencils, pens, stencil set, ruler, steno notebooks

Center Time

Goals   1. The child will learn to organize free play time.
                   2. The child will select one activity at a time.
                   3. The child will be alerted to the beginning and end of an activity

Materials   Sheet of tagboard or cardboard (11″ x 18″)
                   Magnetic strips, hook-and-eye fastener strips, or paper clips
                   Colored pens
                   Construction paper
                   Scissors
                   Glue

Instructions   Make a large chart illustrating the children's activity choices for
                   free time (center time). Under each picture, place a column of
                   magnetic strips (or other fasteners) for attaching children's name
                   tags. Write each child's name or symbol on a small card cut from
                   construction paper. Place mounting on the back. When selecting
                   activity centers, the children place their name tags under the
                   corresponding pictures. When a child is ready to move to another
                   center, demonstrate how to remove the name tag from one area
                   and place it in another.

Art Center   Kitchen Corner   Cozy Corner   Computer

Ashley

Lollipop Patterns

Goals   1. The child will reproduce visual patterns.
2. The child will attend to visual details.

Materials   16 colored circles
16 tongue depressors
Glue
Magnetic strips
Magnetic board or metal surface
Red construction-paper STOP sign
Green construction-paper GO sign

Instructions   Glue each circle to the top of a tongue depressor, and attach a magnetic strip to the back of each circle. On a refrigerator, filing cabinet, or magnetic board, use lollipops to set up a simple pattern for the child to reproduce. Start with three lollipops (red, yellow, red). Gradually increase the length and complexity of the patterns you expect the child to repeat. If necessary, place GO and STOP signs at the beginning and end of the sequence to give a cue.

Variation   Let the child create a pattern. Then take one lollipop away, and ask the child to guess what is missing.

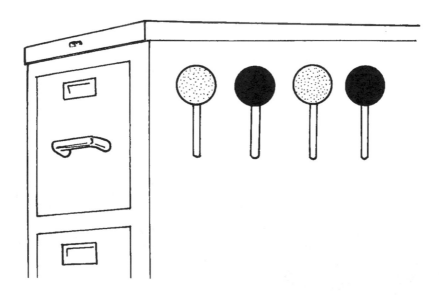

Chalkboard Artist

Goals
1. The child will improve visual-motor coordination.
2. The child will practice social interaction skills while taking turns and waiting for a turn.
3. The child will listen to directions.

Materials
Chalkboard
Large chunks of colored chalk

Instructions
Begin a drawing on the chalkboard. Have the children take turns adding to your picture to complete it. Use colored chalk to add details and stimulate interest, but keep the drawings simple.

Variation
Ask a child to copy a composite design on a small chalkboard.

Magic Star Wand

Goals   1. The child will follow sequential directions.
              2. The child will attend to details.

Materials   Scissors
               Construction paper
               Glue or stapler
               Long straw or thin dowel

Instructions   Cut a star from construction paper. Glue or staple it to the top of the straw or dowel. During circle time, touch the children in turn with the wand, and give each one a direction to follow. ("Touch your nose"; "Clap your hands"; "Wave at me.") Let the children take turns holding the wand and giving directions to their peers. Start with one direction, and gradually increase the number of directions you give at one time.

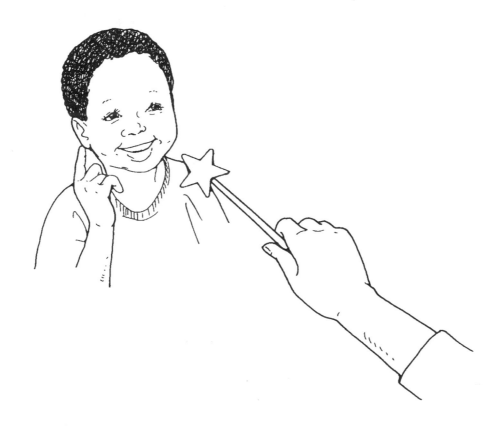

Tinker Bell

Goals   1. The child will learn to focus attention.
2. The child will improve visual tracking ability.

Materials   Flashlights (one for each child and the teacher)

Instructions   Darken the room. Explain to the class that you will be shining the flashlight around the room, and you want them to follow the light by moving just their eyes, not their heads. Shine your flashlight on the chalkboard. Move the light around the room and "spotlight" objects.

Model the correct way to handle the flashlight. Then pass out flashlights to the children. Shine your flashlight on the chalkboard. Ask the children to "catch" the beam from your light with their own beams. Move the light slowly in patterns (circles, up and down, in zigzags), and have the children try to catch the light. When the children catch your light, immediately turn your light off.

Snapshot Models

Goals   1. The child will imitate modeled behaviors.
2. The child will improve attention to tasks.

Materials   Camera and film

Instructions Take pictures of children modeling appropriate classroom behaviors—passing a snack, washing their hands, taking turns, and so on. Display the photos around the classroom at children's eye level. Regularly draw the children's attention to the photos in a positive way. ("Susie, you are washing your hands just like Sarah is in the picture.")

Variation   During story time, ask the children to model good listening. Take their pictures. Before telling another story, pass the pictures around. Encourage the students to comment on what they were doing in the picture. Ask, "How can we tell if someone is a good listener?"

Number Hop

Goals

1. The child will recognize numbers.
2. The child will improve attention for visual cues.
3. The child will control impulsive behaviors.

Materials

Red construction-paper card (9″ x 11″)
Green construction-paper card (9″ x 11″)
Marking pen
2 sets of numeral cards (9″ x 11″)
Chalk tray
Timer

Instructions

Write STOP on the red card and GO on the green card. Place the GO card on the floor to indicate where a child is to stand. Scatter one set of numeral cards face up on the floor, or line them up on the chalk tray. One child stands in front of (or on) the GO card, draws a card from the second numeral set, and moves to stand in front of (or on) the card that matches the number drawn. Use a timer to set a limit on this game, based on each child's attention span. As the activity draws to an end, cue that time is almost over. Give one child the red STOP card, and explain, "When I give Tom a signal, he will put the STOP sign on the floor and the game will be over."

Letter Recognition

Goals
1. The child will attend to color cues highlighting relevant information.
2. The child will recognize differences in letter shapes.

Materials
Large sheets of paper
Felt-tip pens

Instructions
Provide large sheets of paper, and encourage the children to scribble on them. Ask children if they would like to write the letters of their names. Write a child's name, and highlight parts of the letters with different colors. For example, help the child to make a circle and a line for the letters *b, d,* and *p.* Use a different color to highlight the circles in each of these letters.

Go and Stop Circle Cues

Goals
1. The child will attend to color cues highlighting relevant information.
2. The child will start and stop activities at the points indicated by red and green gummed dots.

Materials
Small red and green gummed circles
Large sheet of newsprint
Large felt-tip pen
Toy car

Instructions
Instruct the children that green means GO and red means STOP. Place green and red dots in appropriate places on any task to help the child know where to start and stop. For example, place green dots on lacing string and a tray of beads, and place a storage box with a red dot on it next to the tray. The child works on the lacing activity in the tray; and when the project is finished, the child places the materials in the box.

Variation
Draw a roadway on a large piece of paper. Place a green dot at the beginning and a red one at the end of the roadway. Give the child a toy car to race along the roadway from the green dot to the red dot.

Pretty Picture

Goals
1. The child will improve memory for visual details.
2. The child will improve attention to tasks.

Materials
Large calendar pictures with many details
Scissors
Glue
Tagboard
Laminating material (optional)
Cards numbered from 1 to 3

Instructions
Cut out and mount the pictures on tagboard. (You may wish to laminate them.) Have the children view a picture and name three things they see in it. Turn the picture face down, and hold up the number cards. (This acts as a memory cue.) Ask a child to tell you the three items that were mentioned. As the child names each item, put down one number card. Repeat the activity using the same picture for several days in succession. Observe whether the children's performances improve with repetition.

Shake It

Goals
1. The child will recognize numbers.
2. The child will control impulsive behaviors.
3. The child will improve short-term memory.
4. The child will use a memory device to improve recall.

Materials
Cardboard egg cartons
Large felt-tip pen
Marbles or similar small objects

Instructions
Write a number from 1 to 6 in each section of the egg cartons. Give each child an egg carton and a marble. Each child places the marble inside the egg carton, closes the lid, and shakes the carton. Then the children open their cartons and tell what numbers their marbles landed on.

Variation
Use a rhyme to have children follow different directions, depending on the numbers they end up with.

If you have a number 1,
Point your finger to the sun.

If you have a number 2,
Lift your foot and shake your shoe.

If you have a number 3,
Lift your eyes and look at me.

If you have a number 4,
Make a fist and tap the floor.

If you have a number 5,
Count with me: 1, 2, 3, 4, 5.

If you have a number 6,
Use your hands and mix, mix, mix.
(*Children pantomime mixing batter in a bowl.*)

Large Squares

Goals
1. The child will improve visual memory.
2. The child will recall visual sequences.
3. The child will be able to recall visual details.

Materials
Chalk and chalkboard
Colored construction paper (4-inch squares)
Loops of masking tape

Instructions
Draw a row of 4-inch squares on the chalkboard. Attach a loop of masking tape to the back of each colored square of paper. Place three or four of the colored squares in a row on the chalkboard. Ask the children to observe the order of the squares carefully. Then remove one square. Ask a child to tell you the color of the missing square. Gradually increase the complexity of the task by adding more squares or creating a repeating pattern. Sample arrangements include:

Red, blue, green
Green, green, blue
Red, green, green
Blue, red, green
Blue, green, red
Green, red, blue
Blue, blue, green, green
Red, red, blue, blue

Splash!

Goals   1. The child will improve visual memory.
2. The child will improve visual-motor integration.

Materials   Chalk and chalkboard
Child's large paintbrush
Jar of water
Index cards or cards cut from tagboard
Large felt-tip pens

Instructions   Draw a line or design on the chalkboard. Have the child wet the paintbrush and "paint over" your design (that is, trace over the design with water). Begin with an easy design, such as a curved line, horizontal line, or simple geometric shape.

Variation   Draw a design on a large index card or tagboard. Let the child see the design briefly. Then remove the card, and ask the child to duplicate the design from memory.

What's in the Box?

Goals   1. The child will improve visual memory.
2. The child will improve recall for objects.

Materials   3 different-colored boxes with lids

Instructions   Place one colored box in front of the children. Ask one child to find something of the same color in the room, and to put it in the box. Close the box. Ask the children to remember what is in the box. Repeat this procedure with the remaining two boxes. See whether the children can tell you what's in all three boxes.

Puzzle Time

Goals
1. The child will improve visual memory.
2. The child will attend to visual details.
3. The child will develop concentration skills.

Materials
3-piece wooden puzzles
Box (large enough to hold a puzzle piece)
Can (large enough to hold a puzzle piece)
Square of colored paper (large enough to hold a puzzle piece)

Instructions
Place an assembled wooden puzzle in front of a child. The child removes one piece and puts it in the can, then removes a second piece and puts it in the box. Have the child return both pieces immediately to their correct locations in the puzzle. On the next trial, have the child also remove the third piece and place it on the paper square.

Variation
After the pieces have been placed in the box and can and on the paper square, move the three items around before asking the child to replace the pieces in the puzzle.

Snapshot

Goals 1. The child will use visual cues to recall information.
2. The child will attend to visual details.

Materials Photographs of objects in room

Instructions Present a photograph of an object in the classroom—something the child has seen and is allowed to handle. Ask one child to look carefully at the photo. Then remove the photo, and ask the child to find the actual object in the classroom.

Clothesline

Goals   1. The child will improve memory for visual sequences.
2. The child will recall visual details.

Materials   Light nylon line
Green ribbon
Doll clothes
Clothespins
Basket

Instructions   String up the nylon line to make a clothesline that is within the child's reach. Tie the green ribbon on the left end of the line to signal the child where to start. Tell a story about someone hanging out laundry. Include each item of doll's clothing as you tell the story. As you mention each item, hang it on the line. When all the clothes are hung on the line, explain, "Now the clothes are dry. You can take them down and put them in the clothes basket." When all items have been placed in the basket, ask the child to hand you the pieces in the order they were hanging on the line.

Variation   Rather than using a variety of clothing articles, use four examples of the same item of clothing (such as, four shirts with different patterns).

Picture Patterns

Goals
1. The child will improve visual attention and memory.
2. The child will attend to visual details.
3. The child will develop concentration skills.

Materials
Magazine pictures of people and animals
Large linoleum tile

Instructions
Place the pictures in a left-to-right order on the tile (for example, person, animal, person, animal). Ask the child to reproduce the pattern from memory. The objective is to have the child recognize the pattern (person, then animal). Do not penalize the child for not using the same pictures you used.

Variation
Ask the child to imitate the expressions on the people's faces and make the sound each animal would make.

Fun Box

Goals   1. The child will improve visual memory.
2. The child will attend to visual details.

Materials   Shallow box
3 or 4 objects belonging to one category; for example:
Doll furniture
Plastic fruit
Colored blocks
Dollhouse or other miniature building
Objects that belong in the miniature building

Instructions   Arrange the three (or four) objects in the box. Encourage the children to inspect and name the items in the box. Warn them that you will move the items around and they will have to put them back in order. Then have the children close their eyes while you rearrange the objects. Ask them to open their eyes, tell you which objects you moved, and put the objects back as they were.

Variation   Give the child a dollhouse, toy farm, toy store, or similar building. Put items that belong in the building in the box. Direct the child to perform a variety of tasks. ("Put the bed in the bedroom"; "Put the chair in the kitchen.")

Ring It

This is an excellent activity for teaching counting by fives.

Goals
1. The child will recognize numbers.
2. The child will improve visual memory.
3. The child will sequence numbers.

Materials
Gloves on stretchers, cardboard cutouts of hands,
 or old gloves stuffed with paper
Marking pen
Costume-jewelry rings or small drapery hoops

Instructions
Number the fingers of the gloves from 1 to 5. Have the child place one ring on each finger, then count them out loud. Remove one ring, and ask the child to count again. Add more rings to the glove as the child learns to count beyond 5.

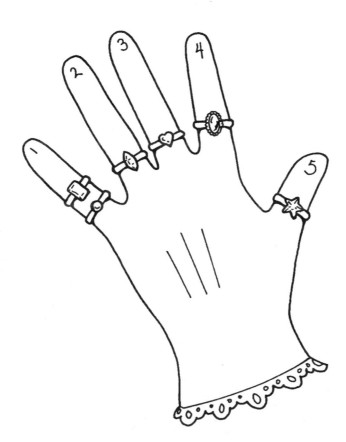

Copy Cat

Goals   1. The child will improve visual-motor memory integration skills.
                   2. The child will follow directions.

Materials   Colored chalk and chalkboard
                       (or marking pens and white board)
                   Colorful writing tools and paper

Instructions   Draw or place a brief pattern of an easy-to-copy design on
                   the board. Use a sequential pattern containing figures you
                   know the children can make (for example, a circle, two dots,
                   a circle, a line, three dots, a square, a line, a circle). Ask the
                   child to copy the design on colorful paper, using marking pens
                   or chalk.

Main Class

Goals   1. The child will listen to directions.
2. The child will control impulsive behaviors.

Materials   None

Instructions Make up a brief story about the children in the group playing at school. Mention each child's name. Tell the children to listen for their names. When a name is called, that child is to clap. Next, have the children stand while you tell another short story. Have them sit down as they hear their names. The last time you tell the story, have the children repeat their names when they hear them.

Variations This game can be used for transition from one activity to another. For example, instruct the children, "When you hear your name, go to the door"; or, "When you hear your name, go to the snack table."

Expand the directions to incorporate basic reasoning and general knowledge. For example, "If you are a boy, clap once when you hear your name. If you are a girl, clap twice."

Number Teams

Goals
1. The child will recognize numbers.
2. The child will follow directions.
3. The child will respond when called on.
4. The child will take turns, wait for a turn, and engage in age-appropriate social interaction.
5. The child will improve memory for auditory information.

Materials
1 or 2 chairs
1 or 2 carpet squares
Number cards
Empty coffee can with plastic lid
Basket of rhythm instruments

Instructions
Place a chair facing the wall. Directly behind the chair, place a carpet square. Next to the carpet square, place a stack of number cards. Have the children form two teams. One child from each team will play in each round of this game.

The child from Team A sits on the chair, while the child from Team B sits on a carpet square behind the first child. The child from Team B takes the top card and claps the number of times shown on the card. The child from Team A calls out the number of claps. If the response is correct, the child from Team A is given the number card to hold. If the response is not correct, the child from Team B keeps the card and taps the appropriate number of times on the floor. Play continues with two more children taking their turns. When everyone has had a turn, the teams switch places.

Variations
Use two chairs and two carpet squares. Place the stack of number cards between the carpet squares. Have the teams compete in a relay race.

Use a coffee can with a plastic lid as a drum, and let the children beat the correct number of times.

Use bells or rhythm sticks to tap out the number.

Tell Me a Story

Goals 1. The child will improve auditory memory.
2. The child will give a specified motor response to an auditory cue.

Materials Record player and record (or tape player and tape) of a short story (2 minutes maximum)

Instructions Play the story. Let each child choose to be a character in the story. Then have the children each create a movement or sign that they can do when they hear their characters. Play the story again. As each character speaks, the corresponding child stands up and makes the appropriate sign.

Variation After the children have heard the story, have them retell it. Each child in turn tells the part of the story that relates to that child's chosen character. Show pictures of the characters as visual cues to help the children remember the story.

Number Drill

Goals
1. The child will improve auditory sequential memory.
2. The child will attend to details.

Materials
Tape recorder and tape
Earphones

Instructions
Record a series of digits on an audiotape. Pause after each set to allow time for the child who is listening to repeat the digits. Begin with sequences of only two digits, and gradually increase the number of digits.

Variations
Ask children who can repeat two digits successfully to repeat the digits backward.

Do the same drill using a series of random words. Say the words aloud, and record both your presentation and the child's response. Play the tape, and encourage the child to evaluate whether the sequence was repeated correctly.

Song Review

Goals   1. The child will review orally the sequence of daily activities.
2. The child will improve auditory memory.

Materials   None

Instructions   After an activity, review the children's experiences by putting the event into song. For example:

> (To the tune of *"She'll Be Comin' 'Round the Mountain"*)
> First we put paint on our brushes, yes we did.
> First we put paint on our brushes, yes we did.
> First we put paint on our brushes,
>   we put paint on our brushes,
> We put paint on our brushes, yes we did.
>
> Next we painted at the easel, yes we did.
> (And so on)
>
> (To the tune of *"You Are My Sunshine"*)
> We painted pictures. We painted pictures.
> We painted pictures in our room.
> We needed paint, we needed brushes.
> We made pictures for our room.

Someone's at the Door

Goals   1. The child will give a specified motor response to an auditory cue.
2. The child will imitate an auditory sequence.
3. The child will control impulsive behavior.

Materials   Buzzer board materials:
Doorbell
Battery
Wires
Block of wood

Instructions   Make a buzzer board by wiring a battery to a doorbell mounted on a block of wood. Tell the child, "Pretend I am coming to your house to play. When I ring the doorbell, you ring back just the way I did." Start with one long ring. Then give two short rings. Remind the child to duplicate your pattern of rings. If the child becomes excited and begins ringing the bell repeatedly, remove it immediately. Continue the game by clapping out an auditory pattern. If the child can get back on task and imitate your clapping, reintroduce the bell. Gradually introduce longer patterns:

One long ring
One short ring
Two short rings
Two long rings
One long, one short ring
One long, two short rings
One short, one long ring
One short, two long rings

Auditory Memory

Copy Cat

Goals 1. The child will complete a series of activities in sequence.
2. The child will maintain attention to task.

Materials None

Instructions Act out an activity that consists of three steps; for example:

1. Get a storybook.
2. Sit on the floor.
3. Open the book.

Verbally describe each step as you do it. Repeat the sequence. Then have the children imitate what you did. Finally, ask questions about the sequence of events. ("What did you do first? Next? Last?")

Variation Act out other activities such as swinging, bouncing a ball, feeding pets, booting a computer.

Draw Me a Picture*

Goals 1. The child will draw a picture given only oral directions.
2. The child will improve listening skills.

Materials Large sheet of newsprint
Large crayons

Instructions Explain to the children, "Today we will draw a picture. I will tell a story, and I want you to close your eyes and imagine seeing the story on television. When I finish the story, make the picture you saw on the television in your mind. Try to draw everything I said in the story. Everything you remember will make me happy."

Tell a brief story of four or five sentences in which you mention specific objects and describe their size, colors, and other attributes. Tell the story slowly, but tell it only once. For example:

> John and Mary are playing in their back yard. There is a fence around the yard. The house is yellow, like the sun. John is swinging high in a swing, and Mary is bouncing a big blue ball.

*Biessman, et al. 1970.

How to Chant

Goals
1. The child will use a mnemonic to aid recall.
2. The child will imitate a verbal rhythm.
3. The child will develop fluency.

Materials   Rhythm instruments

Instructions   Present a chant to one child or to the class. Lead a discussion about the chant. For example, "What did it make you think about?"

Ask the child or children to be your "echoes" or to be "copy cats" and repeat a line of the chant after you. Practice the chant daily. Make up chants for things the children have to remember. Reinforce children who use the chant to help them remember.

Variations   When the children are familiar with the chant, offer other rhythm experiences:

1. Add movement to the chant.
2. Give the children rhythm instruments, and have them keep time or beat to the chant.
3. Chant and clap to the rhythm of the words.
4. Repeat the chant at different volume levels (for example, using a whisper, an "outside voice," and an "inside voice").

Some Chants
Count to 1, count to 2.
Turn around and touch your shoe.
Count to 3, count to 4.
Turn around and touch the floor.
Count to 5, count to 6.
Turn around and touch some sticks.

See the paper. See the wall.
Line up now. March to the hall.

North, South, East, West,
Point to the one you like the best!

Eyes, look up and see me!
Ears, perk up and hear me!
Tell your eyes to look, look, look!
Tell your ears to hear, hear, hear!
Look! Hear! Far! Near!
Eyes and ears will make it clear.*

Roll the ball, that's our game.
My name is _____. What's your name?*

*Herzog and Gibbs 1989.

Rhythm Band

Goals
1. The child will improve auditory sequential memory.
2. The child will improve motor expression.
3. The child will attend to auditory directions.
4. The child will control impulsive behaviors.

Materials
Box of rhythm instruments
Red STOP sign
Green GO sign

Instructions
Place the rhythm instruments in front of the children. Model playing each one; then let the children try them. Let each child choose an instrument to play. Explain that when you hold up the GO sign, they may start playing; and when you hold up the STOP sign, they are to stop playing immediately. Show the GO and STOP signs alternately, and remind the children as needed how they are to respond.

Anticipating the Refrain

Goals
1. The child will anticipate future events.
2. The child will control impulsive behavior.

Materials
Books or chants with repetitive refrains, such as *Drummer Hoff, Three Billy Goats Gruff,* and *Bear Hunt*

Instructions
Frequently read books with repetitive refrains. Encourage the children to chant the refrain along with you. When they have learned the refrain, pause before you read it, and encourage the children to say it aloud.

"Simon Says" and "Red Light, Green Light"

Goals   1. The child will control motor responses.
2. The child will start and stop on signal.

Materials   Red STOP sign
Green GO sign

Instructions   Play these well-known children's games. In "Simon Says," one player (Simon) gives directions to the other players, who follow the direction only if it begins with, "Simon says, . . ." If the children have difficulty with this game initially, use the phrases, "Simon says" and "Simon does not say" with the directions to give them a cue. Eventually drop "Simon does not say."

In "Red Light, Green Light," one player (IT) stands on one side of the room. The other players stand at a starting line on the opposite side of the room. The children move when IT calls out, "Green light," but they stop immediately when IT calls out, "Red light." Any child who moves after the "red light" signal must go back to the starting line. The object is to be the first player to reach IT. For children who need an additional cue, hold up STOP and GO signs as you call out "Red light" and "Green light." The children may move by running, hopping, skipping, or jumping. To increase the difficulty of the game, give instructions for the players to move in different ways on each turn.

Impulse Activities

Goals
1. The child will control motor responses.
2. The child will start and stop on a signal.

Materials
Plastic container
Plastic cup (same volume as the container)
Liquid
Sand
Rice

Instructions
Fill the container with liquid. Have the children practice pouring the liquid from the container into a cup without spilling. Have them repeat the exercise with a container filled with sand, then with rice. Once they have mastered pouring back and forth, have them start and stop pouring on your command.

Variation
Draw a line around the inside of the cup, and ask the child to fill the cup only to the line.

Think Tank

Goals   1. The child will learn to control impulsive behavior.
2. The child will respond to verbal cues.

Materials   None

Instructions   Have the children put their hands in their pockets or sit on them. Ask a basic-knowledge question such as, "What color is a carrot?" Then say, "Hands?" Children who know the answer raise their hands. When you say, "Answer," the children respond simultaneously. After several repetitions, begin calling on individual children to answer. Reward and reinforce children for raising their hands.

Turn It Over!

Goals
1. The child will control impulsive behavior.
2. The child will understand time constraints.

Materials
Letter cards, Scrabble® game tiles, or cutout letters
Timer

Instructions
Place three letter cards or game tiles face down in front of the child. Set a timer for 15 seconds. Ask the child to turn over as many letters as possible before the timer rings. When time has run out, have the child name the letters that were turned over. Gradually increase the number of letters and the time allotted, as appropriate for individual children.

Eyes Front

Goals

1. The child will become less distracted.
2. The child will focus on a task.

Materials

Overhead projector and screen
Cutout geometric shapes

Instructions

Make sure that the children recognize and can name the shapes you are using. Place three shapes in a row, and project them on the screen. Ask the children to look carefully at the shapes, and then have them cover their eyes. Remove one shape. Count to three slowly. Then say, "Eyes front. What's missing?" Have one child stand up to answer and another child replace the missing shape.

Variations

Use animal cutouts or letters of the alphabet.

Have the children name all three items in order from left to right.

Hands, Toes, Faces

Goals
1. The child will listen to directions.
2. The child will reduce impulsive behaviors.

Materials   None

Instructions   Sit in a circle with three children. To keep restless hands and feet still, you may wish to have them sit with legs outstretched and hands resting on their knees. Tell the children that when you call out a body part, they are to look at that part and touch it.

Variation   When you call out a child's name and a body part, the other children all turn and watch as the individual child touches the body part named.

Slow Motion

Goals
1. The child will control impulsive actions.
2. The child will follow visual/verbal directions.

Materials   None

Instructions   Teacher begins by doing in pantomime something that is "slow" (acting like an elephant, a snake, a feather floating in the air, a bubble). The children try to guess what the teacher is miming. When a child guesses the correct answer, all stand and act out what they saw. The child who answered takes the next turn.

Variation   Act out simple tasks in slow motion (putting on a coat, clearing crayons from the table, lining up for recess). Ask a child to imitate the action.

Cartoon Character Match-Up

Goals   1. The child will control impulsive actions.
                   2. The child will follow visual/verbal directions.

Materials   Colorful pictures of Barney® (or other cartoon character) in a
                       variety of action poses
                   Plastic whistle
                   Bell
                   Instant camera and film

Instructions   Show pictures of Barney® (or other popular cartoon character)
                   in different poses. Encourage children to model the poses.
                   Select a student to blow the whistle. Tell the children that
                   when they hear the whistle, they must "freeze" like the
                   character. When the bell rings, they can move freely around
                   the room again. The use of the bell and whistle help children
                   to model stop and start skills.

Variation   Take pictures of classmates on the playground. Ask the
                   children to model their own classmates' poses.

Chapter 6

The Role of the Early Childhood Teacher

I have taught every grade level from preschool to high school. My favorite area to teach, however, will always be early childhood. I enjoy the challenge of being one of the first significant role models in a child's life. It is an important role and one that must be taken with great dedication and perseverance. I believe that the role of the teacher is literally that of an "environmental engineer," one who arranges the learning environment for the child's success and who encourages learning through that environment (Jones 1994).

The teacher or caregiver offers opportunities for children to express their ideas and participate in social and emotional experiences. The materials we provide or omit from the environment shape the children's play and send them a message about what we value and support. Through this interactive participation, children begin to develop adaptive and independent living behaviors. The environment we create may be the key in helping them to develop a natural motivation for learning.

For most young children, play and busy activity is a way of life. For children with attention disorders, however, this busy activity may be accompanied by difficulties with impulsivity, turn taking, sequencing, visual/motor/memory integration, and short-term memory. To help children with special concerns, the teacher needs to keep in mind the developmental stages of attention and the individual needs of each child. Therefore, the selection of activities and materials is extremely important. It involves decisions about the kinds of interests, motivation, and skills we want each child to develop.

The Role of the Classroom Teacher

1. Be aware of the normal developmental stages of attention.
2. Use a checklist to establish a baseline for behaviors (such as the *Conners, ACTeRS,* or *Yale*).
3. Ask another professional to observe the child, using the same measure.
4. Communicate with the family. Ask family members to use a checklist to observe behaviors at home.
5. Identify the child's strengths.
6. Employ behavioral strategies.
7. Employ educational interventions.

Guidelines for Intervention: Three to Six Years

The educational environment (center, class, or preschool) offers young children opportunities to interact with their peers and caregivers, to engage in meaningful experiences, and to develop their cognitive skills. The following sections will provide a variety of activities and opportunities for independent and guided play as well as free-time play.

Encouraging Play

Children's desire and need to play has been recognized throughout history (Borstelmann 1983; Bruner, et. al. 1976). Children are curious about the world. They reach out to touch it, taste it, and explore it. They play alone or with others, with things, and with ideas. Elkind (1993) believes we should encourage play for its own sake because it provides an avenue for children to express themselves in personal ways. He states, "Play is not the child's work, and work is hardly child's play" (29). Play may be one of the most profound expressions of human nature and one of the greatest innate resources for learning and invention (Bronson 1996). Play should be part of the fun in life—and who better to enjoy play than a child? But what happens to the overactive child who is always too noisy, too rough, and just too out of control? Who invites this child to play? What does a teacher do with a child who doesn't play well?

Play is difficult for children with ADHD because they are impulsive and often can't wait for a turn. They become overstimulated and "overpower" their playmates. They lose interest in the game and forget to follow the rules. While the child with ADHD may have a good time playing, nobody else has much fun (Ziffer 1990).

The teacher, therapist, and caregiver can help the child with ADHD to develop skills that permit success within play. The use of physical role modeling with the game or activity is helpful. The adult can act out how to select the game, how to ask others to play, and how to play like a "good friend." The child with ADHD can step through this role play before an actual playmate is invited to join the game.

Select games and activities based on the key principles of brevity, variety, and structure (see page 66). Choose games that have novelty or uniqueness rather than repetitive and similar steps. Use games that are concrete and simple in format and can be completed in a short period of time.

1. When introducing play activities, start with a slow, systematic approach. Help the child play well with one activity; then move to playing that activity with a trusted sibling or parent; then invite a special friend to join the play.

2. Model appropriate language to use when playing. ("Luis, friends will like it when you say 'Great job,' the way you said to me when we were playing. It makes a friend want to play with you.")

3. Be specific in your praise. Show the child what you want, not what you don't want. ("You know how to be a friend, Doug. You let me go first in picking a game piece. Thank you!")

4. Ensure success. Ziffer (1990) suggests that when helping an ADHD child learn to play more appropriately, each play experience should be a successful one. He encourages the caregiver to plan out each play activity so that it "fits" the style of each unique child.

5. Help the child to develop an interest in which he or she can become an expert. Others will seek out the child to hear about an interesting collection or hobby. Some hobbies and activities that may interest children with ADHD are collecting baseball cards, rocks, postcards, patches, or action figures; building models or Legos®; working with wood; sculpting; performing magic tricks, puppetry, juggling, dramatic plays; and taking photographs.

Daily Presentation of Activities

Children with ADHD respond best when formal, structured, and focused activities are followed by informal, unstructured, and unfocused activities (Goldstein and Goldstein 1990).

1. When the schedule calls for an active period followed by a more structured one, design a "winding down" exercise to smooth the transition to a formal lesson. Design activities to go from unstructured to slightly structured to structured.

2. Use center time (which provides a variety of activities within the classroom) as an effective transition between a structured, sit-down time and a more active, unstructured time. (See pages 108–109 for hands-on activities that contain ideas for center time.)

3. Alternate children between centers that require minimal sit-down time and more active centers to create a balance of learning levels (Holman, Banet, and Weikart 1979).

Enhancing Memory

Attention difficulties impair the memory ability of many children with ADHD; this, in turn, affects their academic performance. Children who have difficulty concentrating may not be able to process several thoughts simultaneously or be able to store and retrieve that information quickly. Memory difficulties can impair their ability to recall letters of the alphabet (recognition memory) despite repeated instruction. Other memory weaknesses can include number recall (phone numbers, addresses, and so on) and recall of letter formations. It is not unusual to encounter students in whom one or more of these retrieval processes is slow, variable, or inaccurate (Levine 1987b).

There are two types of memory that appear to be part of the profile of a child with ADHD: short-term and long-term memory. *Short-term memory* is a process of accumulating information quickly while concentrating on it. Levine (1987b) identifies it as *primary memory*. *Long-term memory* is the process whereby information is stored after it has been repeated and processed with thoughtful attention. It is the vast accumulation of what we know.

Children who are distracted by either visual or auditory factors typically have difficulty with short-term memory for visual and auditory information (Silver 1989). This difficulty is characterized by a "now they have it, now they don't" phenomenon (Telzrow and Speer 1986b). Children with poor short-term memories often require multiple repetitions to retain information that a developmentally average child retains with minimal reiteration. If you are concerned about a child's lack of recall, you may want to introduce compensatory memory strategies as an intervention. Children with ADHD often have excellent long-term memory. They recall the unique and the unusual, not the same and the similar.

Memory Strategies

1. Employ multimodality techniques (visual, auditory, tactile) when introducing information that requires short-term memory skills.

2. Remember the three principles of *brevity, variety,* and *structure* when presenting.

3. Use mnemonics to enhance recall. A *mnemonic* is a device or formula that aids one in remembering. Three types of mnemonics appear to work best for children with attention problems:

   - Rhythm (rhyme, beat, or chant)
   - Categorization or clustering (visual cues that highlight chunks of information)
   - Association (making connections with previously learned material)

4. Provide adequate time for the child to respond to, review, and recall information.

5. Gradually increase the number of items to recall until you reach the child's limit. Then return immediately to the level at which the child was successful.

6. Before beginning instruction, discuss what will be presented. Review key points during the lesson, and repeat them afterward.

7. As academic work becomes more complex, continually reinforce and reassure the child.

8. Provide a visual model for children to refer to throughout the lesson. Consistently offer it as a reminder in similar activities. For example, attach a number line to a tray where a child is working with counting disks.

Pre-Reading Experiences

Research on early literacy development has provided considerable insight into the precursors of becoming successful readers and writers (Teale 1978; Morrow and Smith 1990; Beach 1996). Current research indicates that the factor correlating most highly with a child's learning to read easily in primary school is whether she or he has been read to frequently as a very young child (Strickland and Taylor 1989; McLane and McNamee 1990). It is this close sharing of a book between a child and a caring adult that helps the child grow to love and bond with books (Strickland and Taylor 1989). According to the Carnegie Foundation report, *The Basic School: A Community of Learners* (Boyer 1995), kindergarten teachers surveyed stated that as many as 35% of kindergarten children come to school unprepared for formal education. Making books an integral part of a young child's life is a goal that every childhood program would attain.

More than half of the children diagnosed with ADHD will fall at least one grade level behind in reading by age twelve, often in spite of having normal intelligence (Minde, et al. 1971). They have difficulty concentrating on rote drills, such as learning the alphabet; they may appear to be inattentive; and they tend to "tune out" during reading activities that require sustained attention.

Poor reading ability is a major cause of academic underachievement for middle-school and high-school students with ADHD (Shaywitz, et al. 1994). The results of the Rowe and Rowe study (1992) indicated that inattentiveness may play an even stronger role in influencing poor reading achievement than do other factors.

It is difficult to predict at an early age how academically troubled a child will be. Because early intervention appears to be successful, however, providing strategies for developing reading readiness skills would be expected to benefit the child. Durkin (1966a) suggested that beginning to read early is of special value for children who are language delayed or slower in developing. The researcher's hypothesis was that introducing reading activities earlier gave these children a longer time to acquire needed skills.

Children with attention deficit disorders often have difficulty listening to a story, focusing their attention on the page, and remembering it. Extensive investigations have been conducted on the relationship between hearing stories read and later reading ability, although there is limited research specifically dealing with children who are attention delayed. Research findings generally indicate that children who were read to frequently accumulated more background information and had more interest in learning to read (Bower 1976; Chomsky 1972; Durkin 1966b). A unique study of the effect of oral reading on children with language delays was undertaken by Degler (1979), who examined wordless books—those in which the "reader" must provide a text based on the pictures. Degler concluded that children's exposure to wordless books correlated significantly with improvement in language. The primary factor was the participation of an adult in relating the pictures to the child and in answering questions.

In studies of four- to five-year-old children who were developmentally delayed, Catts and Kamhi (1986) suggested that the children's attention should be drawn to the actual sounds of words. They recommended reading aloud in general, as well as reciting nursery rhymes and reading stories that contain frequent repetition. They found that this training may also improve children's word recognition skills.

Cohen (1968) studied children whose teachers read to them in class every day for one school year. The stories were introduced in order of increasing difficulty and were accompanied by followup comprehension questions. Cohen concluded that regular exposure to stories significantly improved oral language and reading skills. Also interesting was the reversal of a trend toward reading failure in several of the children.

The results of these studies generally support that reading aloud to children makes a significant difference in their oral language and later reading achievement. Although the research to date has focused on children with language delays, the findings imply that a child who has strong auditory skills but limited attention to the printed word also will benefit. Exposure to wordless or low-text picture books, recitation of nursery rhymes, and listening activities in the early years should be of special value for the child who is at risk for future reading difficulty.

Enhancing Reading Readiness

1. Provide a variety of books that are appropriate for the children's ages and stages of development.
2. Use books with content that reflects objects and events in the children's environment.
3. Be sure that books are child-size, durable (plastic coated or covered), and brightly colored.
4. Provide books with high-interest and imaginative content.
5. Readiness goals should mirror the children's interests and cultural identities.
6. In the book area of the room, have soft, comfortable furniture to encourage sitting or lying while reading. Locate the book area in the least distracting corner of the room.
7. Place books at the children's eye level on low shelves or in boxes with the front covers facing out.

Teaching Activities

1. Model the correct way of handling books and returning them to the shelf.
2. Encourage, praise, and reinforce correct handling of books.
3. Display pictures of characters from children's books, and encourage children to associate them with the pictures in their books.

4. Play fantasy games that involve the characters in the books, using dolls or stuffed animals for the characters.

5. Provide earphones for playing audio recordings of favorite stories. Let children tape-record themselves telling stories or describing events in a book.

6. As you play with children in the room, draw their attention to a character's picture. Name the character, and challenge children to tell you stories from the books about that character.

7. When you hand a book to a child, read the title aloud and relate it to something the child knows. ("Here's a book about your favorite color. It's *Harold and the Purple Crayon*.")

8. Photograph daily events or favorite friends to make a picture book. Look through the book with the child, and find one page that attracts a particular interest. Name the picture, and ask the child to talk about it. Cover the photo and see if the child can remember what was in the photo.

9. At first, have the child lie on the floor with the book at eye level. Later, sit with the child on the floor, and place the book on the child's lap as you turn the pages.

10. Begin with wordless picture books. Ask the child to name pictures on the page. Advance to having the child describe what might be happening in the pictures.

11. Let the child select a favorite book, and then choose one page of the book. Ask the child to name something on the page. (Draw attention to the book, if necessary, by pointing to and tapping the picture or by using a small puppet.) Close the book, mark the page, and say to the child, "Close your eyes, and think about what was on the page." Then have the child open the book and find the picture. Gradually have the child name more objects on the page.

12. Introduce books with very simple story lines.

13. Point to the printed words as you read aloud, and let the child know that these are the words you are reading. ("These words tell me what the bear is doing.")

14. Hold the book so the child can see the pages. Let the child point to and touch the objects you name.

15. Ask children to draw their own stories. Bind the stories together and place them on the bookshelf.

16. Use the child's name in place of the main character to make a new version of the story.

17. Talk about real versus make-believe characteristics. ("Can lions really talk?")

18. Use bibliotherapy—books with a therapeutic message—to help children cope with their own challenges and to increase their self-esteem. (See page 166 for a list of books for bibliotherapy.)

Teacher Resources

Books Written Especially for Younger Children About ADD

Corman, C., and E. Trevino. *Eukee the Jumpy, Jumpy Elephant*. Rockville, MD: Woodbine House, 1995.

Galvin, M. *Otto Learns About His Medicine: A Story About Medication for Hyperactive Children*. New York: Imagination Press, 1988.

Levine, M. *All Kinds of Minds*. Cambridge, MA: Educators Publishing Service, 1992.

Lotz, K. *Can't Sit Still*. New York: Dutton Children's Books, 1993.

Moss, D. *Shelley, The Hyperactive Turtle*. Rockville, MD.: Woodbine House, 1989.

Shapiro, L. *Sometimes I Drive My Mom Crazy, But I Know She's Crazy About Me*. King of Prussia, PA: The Center for Applied Psychology, 1993.

Stories for Short Attention Spans

Asch, F. *Sand Cake*. New York: Parents' Magazine Press, 1978.

Barrett, J. *Animals Should Definitely Not Wear Clothing*. New York: Atheneum, 1970.

Brown, M. *Finger Rhymes*. New York: E. P. Dutton, 1980. (*Suitable for chanting*)

Cooke, T., and H. Osenbury. *So Much*. Cambridge, MA: Candlewick, 1994.

Crews, D. *Freight Train*. New York: Greenwillow Books, 1978.

Dale, P. *The Elephant Tree*. New York: Putnam, 1991.

Hayes, S. *Clap Your Hands: Finger Rhymes*. New York: Lothrop, Lee, and Shepard, 1988. (*Suitable for chanting*)

Joose, B., and B. Lavallee. *Mama, Do You Love Me?* San Francisco: Chronicle, 1991.

Moore, I. *Six-Dinner Sid*. New York: Simon & Schuster, 1991.

Shulevits, U. *Dawn*. New York: Farrar, Strauss & Giroux, 1974.

Zion, G. *Harry and the Lady Next Door*. New York: Harper, 1960.

Books for Bibliotherapy

Bang, M. *Ten, Nine, Eight*. New York: Mulberry, 1939.

Briggs, R. *The Bear*. New York: Random House, 1994.

Brown, M. W., and G. Williams. *Wait Till the Moon Is Full*. New York: HarperTrophy, 1948.

Cannon, J. *Stellaluna*. New York: Harcourt Brace, 1993.

Haas, I. *The Maggie B*. New York: Macmillan, 1975.

Issacs, A. *Swamp Angel*. New York: Dutton, 1993.

Lester, J., and J. Pinkey. *John Henry*. New York: Dial Press, 1994.

Pfister, M. *The Rainbow Fish*. New York: North-South Books, 1992.

Solotow, C., and T. Hoban. *The Moon Was the Best*. New York: Greenwillow, 1993.

Spinelli, E. *Somebody Loves You, Mr. Hatch*. New York: Bradbury, 1991.

Stevenon, J. *The Worst Person's Christmas*. New York: Greenwillow, 1991.

Weiss, L. *Funny Feet!* New York: Franklin Watts, 1978.

White Deer of Autumn and C. Grigg. *The Great Change*. Hillsboro, OR: Beyond Words, 1992.

Yolen, J., and J. Schoenherr. *Owl Moon*. New York: Philomel, 1987.

Commercial Games for Active Children: Six and Older

Concentration®. A memory game with pictures (Milton Bradley)

Electronic Simon™. A battery-operated, color-coded game to enhance memory skills (Coleco)

Guess Who®. A game of visual details (Milton Bradley)

Kat Tracks™. Counting and following simple directions (Educational Insights)

Listening Lotto™. Audiotape that encourages matching sounds with pictures on a lotto board (Educational Insights)

Make-A-Game™. A kit to make your own game (Childswork/Childsplay)

Soft, plush-like gym balls, bats, and footballs

Sesame Street® Games for Growing™. Beginning reading and sound symbol games (International Games)

Somebody®. Simple anatomy (Aristoplay)

Chapter 7

Helping Parents Understand Their Child with ADD

One night I decided to treat my family to Swedish meatballs, which I hadn't made in a long time. My first step? Get out the recipe box and search for the recipe card my mother had written years ago. Similarly, if we decide to build a new patio in our backyard, I'll be off to the library to get books on landscaping, because I know I will find a great plan there. My new computer came with a CD "tour guide" of its own just to lead me through the complex instructions of setting up my unit. Instructions are an important part of most of our lives. As the adage goes, "If all else fails, read the instructions!"

But what happens when the subject is parenting and I am struggling to understand how I should "handle the job"? What set of instructions is available for parents when they begin to raise their children? In particular, what guidelines are there for the parent of a hyperactive child who may require even more complex instructions and guidance? One mother said to me, "The teachers want me to organize Justin's book bag every day at home before he leaves for school, but they don't know how hard it is for me to organize my own things. I can't find my checkbook, I've lost my own car keys, and I can't remember where I put my glasses. How can I help Justin?"

Children with attention disorders are, at best, frustrating to parents and, at worst, nightmares that cause the family to focus its entire energy on coping with the behavior. Inattention, impulsiveness, and overactivity—the primary traits associated with attention deficit disorder—cause these children to interrupt lives around them and produce distress within families. Parents of these children frequently report feelings of depression and anxiety. These parents are also more likely than parents of normally developing children to experience stressful events, such as marital difficulties, divorce, and hospitalization (Bower 1988).

169

Attention deficit disorder is *not* caused by dysfunctional parenting; however, dealing with these difficult behaviors can challenge the most stable relationships and affect the dynamics of the entire family unit. Parents often report that from birth, this child was colicky, difficult to console, and restless. First-time parents are more likely than other parents to feel inadequate, distressed, and in some cases, like failures, because they do not have other child-rearing experiences for comparison. Parents with other children who are functioning normally may feel troubled by their inability to cope effectively with this child. The child's behavior (or, more likely, misbehavior) becomes an ongoing issue in school and with extended family members. As a child matures and the problems persist, parents' desires and dreams for the child deteriorate into disappointment and anger. Parents of children with attention deficit disorder should be encouraged to seek help for the child, themselves, and their entire family. They need to know that a variety of interventions and treatment plans is available. Support groups and services are available throughout the United States. Children and Adults with Attention Deficit Disorder (CH.A.D.D.) is the nation's leading organization dedicated to improving the lives of individuals with ADD and of those who care for them. Through support and advocacy, public and professional education, and encouragement of scientific and educational research, CH.A.D.D. works to ensure that those with ADHD reach their inherent potential. See page 178 for the national headquarters address and telephone number.

Five Steps Forward

The first and foremost step for parents who suspect that their child has attention problems is to seek professional assistance and advice. Medical providers—pediatricians, family physicians, and diagnostic specialists—are the resource most families usually consult. Counselors, educational specialists, psychologists, and specialized evaluation centers are other excellent starting places. If parents are unsure where to seek advice, encourage them to seek professionals who are experienced in attention disorders and are conversant about the resources available in the school and the community.

The second step is for parents to learn about the characteristics of attention deficit and how this disorder affects their child's life (not to mention their own). In their day-to-day lives, these children face multiple problems. The majority experience ongoing frustration and confrontation. These negative experiences erode their self-esteem and motivation. By understanding the disorder, parents can help their child to rebuild a sense of self.

The third step is for parents to consider what has occurred in a child's life and to examine parenting skills that will help this child cope. Research indicates that treatment for attention deficit is long-term and that there is no quick solution. Thus, management of ADD will be lifelong. Professionals can offer information to parents regarding management plans and provide up-to-date lists of community resources.

The fourth step is to become involved. The parent progresses beyond dealing with the child's day-to-day behavior to become an informed advocate for the child and other children with this problem. Involvement begins with identifying knowledgeable professionals and experimenting with the techniques they suggest. Parents then initiate treatment and behavioral strategies that make a long-term difference. The parent also will begin working with the school personnel to develop an effective educational plan. Finally, through involvement in support groups and advocacy, families can share ideas for coping with this disorder and ensure quality treatment for people with attention deficit.

The fifth step is to develop a positive attitude. The family needs to believe that their efforts will make a difference and that eventually this child, who is so difficult, will develop into a positive, productive individual. Although it is true that children with attention deficit are at high risk for academic and social difficulty, they also have the potential for high achievement with a positive "we can do it" attitude. Parents can empower their children to cope with an attention disorder and increase their chances for success. By developing this child's strengths and accommodating for weaknesses, professionals and parents are beginning to provide for change. Parents are fortunate when their need for support, management strategies, and effective treatment plans are met because, through these interventions, they will be able to help the unique child survive and thrive. In their book, *Hyperactive Children Grown Up* (1986), authors Weiss and Heichman interviewed a group of individuals who had gone through the Canadian Mental Health Services. The authors asked them what had made a significant difference in their lives with attention deficit disorder. They all responded in a similar way: "My parents. They never gave up on me."

Opportunities for Parent Education

Under IDEA (the Individuals with Disabilities Education Act), parents are empowered to contact local public schools to see whether preschool programs are offered for children with developmental concerns. Local school-district "Round-up" or "Child Find Programs" for children with special needs may be the place to start with the child with attention concerns, a language disability, or other disabling condition. For three- and four-year-old children who are eligible, an individualized education program (IEP) within the public school is required to be developed in conjunction with the parents. The type and amount of additional parent involvement and the provision of adult support is dictated by the needs of the child and the parents, and by the resources available to the program. The child with attention deficit may not be eligible for public school programs when no other disabling condition is present.

Parents of young children are usually concerned and anxious to provide for their child's education in a positive manner. Because of the children's age, the parents spend a great deal of time with their children and usually are eager to learn techniques to help improve their child's behavior, communication, and self-help skills.

The parent of a hyperactive child may find it difficult to find a preschool program that is conducive to learning and growth. Preschools that use developmentally appropriate curriculum will be helpful to the parent. Some parents find their child does best in a home-centered day-care or preschool program where the ratio of child to caregiver is low and provides more one-on-one experiences. During the toddler years, the active, spirited child will need more than the usual amount of modeling of appropriate behavior and structure. Therefore, children with ADHD benefit from lower child-to-adult ratios.

Throughout the community, there are various opportunities for helping parents learn about their child's behavior and the symptoms of attention deficit disorder. Some of these resources include:

- Local CH.A.D.D. group meetings
- Community college courses on active children
- Commercially offered parent classes such as Active Parenting
- Parent classes offered at mental health clinics and facilities
- Parent classes offered at religious centers, public schools, and HeadStart centers

There are numerous books available on parenting a child with attention concerns. See page 177 for lists of these books and videotapes.

See "Fact Sheet: Attention Deficit Disorder" (pages 180–183). This brief overview is made available for use with parents and other concerned individuals who want general information on ADHD. You may reproduce this handout. It is an excellent resource material to have available for parents.

Helping Parents Understand
Their Child's Challenge

One parent told me, "I always knew my child was more hyperactive than most other children his age. I just didn't want the preschool teacher to tell me! I was hoping this behavior would go away in preschool." When a concerned preschool teacher or early childhood caregiver begins to observe behavior such as hyperactivity, impulsiveness, or inattention to daily routines, it is time to involve the parents to determine the possible nature of the observed behaviors. It takes a person who cares and acts professionally to express any concerns gracefully. The parent needs to feel the positive nature of the observations and consider the expression of the caregiver. A master teacher/caregiver will always start a parent conference by sharing the positive behaviors he or she has observed, and then introducing the areas of need in a respectful manner.

"Jesse has such talent with Legos®. He enjoys building and planning wonderful creations! Did you see the car he made on Monday? Jesse knows how to design without looking at the directions. This is such a talent for Jesse! Does he like to build at home, also? . . . One area concerns me. Jesse has great difficulty when we come into the circle to begin to plan our day. It is hard for him to listen to my directions, and he has a challenge sitting and listening as other students share their comments. Have you seen this at home, also? . . . I'm trying to help Jesse by allowing him to hold some plastic string when we sit in a group. This seems to keep his active fingers busy while listening. I am careful to have him sit across from me for good modeling. I am recording the things I am trying, and I'm watching to see how he responds."

This introduction to the behaviors the teacher has observed is stated in a concrete, positive manner. It allows the teacher to share information with the parent regarding what is considered appropriate behavior at this age. It lets the parent see that the teacher is trying a variety of strategies and is willing to hear what is tried at home. This starts conversations about behaviors in a very forthright and caring manner. This strategy is particularly appropriate for the parent who has low expectations of the child and believes the child is not capable of success. See "Common Problems of Children with Attention Disorders" (pages 184–185). This chart is helpful to bring to a parent meeting to explain and review atypical behaviors of children with ADHD.

At times, it may be important to demonstrate to the parent what is actually going on in the classroom. Children with attentional problems experience their greatest difficulty in the classroom, because teachers require listening skills within a group and following of sequential directions in a multistep fashion. At home, the child may not have experienced more than one-on-one or two-to-one instruction. Therefore, some of the behaviors observed in a group situation will not have been observed as readily by the parents at home. Invite the parents to visit the classroom, participate fully in the day, and observe firsthand what the teacher has seen. Videotaping the children also is an excellent teaching intervention. Parents who are unable to visit in the school can learn a great deal about the school day and its demands, and their child's responses, by observing a tape of the entire class but focusing on the specific child. Such a tape can be the "groundwork" for discussing helpful strategies and a way to point out interventions that the teacher is using in the classroom. The video also could be used as a tool to help parents learn to model the interventions in their own home.

This information from a well-meaning teacher can mean a great deal to many parents of children with attention deficits. At times, parents with young, active children are such a target for negative comments regarding their child's behavior that they are embarrassed to take them out in public and feel personally responsible for their inappropriate behaviors. One parent told me she asked herself, "What am I doing wrong to have a child like this?" Her own mother constantly told her it was her fault that the child was so active. When I began to work with this parent, my focus was to help her understand that her son's behaviors were the result of a disorder that was present from birth, and that there were ways she could make a difference by learning some successful techniques. It was helpful to show her that ADHD is a disability as much as hearing or visual impairment. I called it a "hidden disability." I wanted her to be educated about ADHD so that she could learn to be on her child's side as his advocate. I realized my support to her was critical, so we worked together to achieve small steps, one by one, thereby reviving her confidence and strengthening the idea of being her son's advocate. As this parent grew in her own education about the disorder and became skilled in behavior strategies and management of her son, I invited her to speak at one of my evening university classes to share the important things that she had learned and the things that she had accomplished as a parent advocate. Two years later, the woman's mother wrote her a letter apologizing for her earlier negative comments and thanking her for working so hard for her grandson's success. See pages 186–189, "Coping with Attention Deficit Disorder." This handout can be a tool for parents to develop their own skills to be their child's advocate.

See pages 190–193, "Coping with Your Child's Behavior," for helpful strategies. Parents can use these guidelines to create a successful environment for their child with ADHD.

Taking a Child to Public Places

When I began working with the young mother referred to above, she had expressed her concern and embarrassment about taking her child into public places. She was unable to control his overt behavior and was concerned about the negative comments she had received from people around her. When a parent is worried about taking the child out to public places because of the child's behavior, the caregiver or teacher can offer support. This professional can suggest techniques for helping the child learn how to plan and develop self-control. These methods include setting up rules before entering the public place, agreeing with the child on an incentive for compliance with the rules, and establishing a disciplinary response for noncompliance. The caregiver can model this management procedure and show how it can be used in the future. See pages 194–197, "Taking Your Child to Public Places." This outline shows a parents' management plan to use when taking the child on an outing.

Does a Child Outgrow Hyperactivity?

When will a child be the most hyperactive in his or her life span? Between the ages of infancy and about eight years of age will be the most active years for a child with ADHD. At one time, physicians and practitioners believed that children would grow out of hyperactivity. Now we know they do not grow out of it; rather, as the child ages we see the overt behaviors identified earlier develop more into a restless presentation. The child begins to cope with the high activity level and finds ways to abate it. Thus, the preschooler who darts from one thing to another in the playroom and falls out of his chair develops into a fidgety elementary child; and by adolescence, we observe restless behavior. The visible symptoms may change, but children do not outgrow attention disorders.

Providing a Safe Environment

All children deserve the opportunity to grow up in an environment that is secure and protected. Children with ADHD often challenge even the most secure environments because of their high activity levels. Their physical, impulsive nature may bring injury to themselves when they are younger because of their seemingly fearless manner.

As preschoolers, they will be the children who jump off the curb without listening to directions, who run into the water in a ditch without thought of its depth, and the youngsters who grab the liquid bleach to see what it tastes like without any preconceived thought about what might happen. Anticipating these sudden outbursts of energy, the parents of an overactive preschooler will need to protect the child's environment. Removing items that could be unsafe and thinking ahead to what might be a distraction is critical. See pages 198–199, "Keeping Your Child Safe." This handout is offered as a reminder to parents that we must be constantly alert around a young, hyperactive, impulsive child, and we need to childproof the child's environment whenever we can.

Guidelines for Teachers and Therapists: Helping Parents Cope

There are a variety of strategies and interventions that therapists and caregivers can use to help support the parents of the child with attentional concerns.

1. Keep note cards on the child's daily progress and problems and how these problems were handled. See Behavior Observation Cards, pages 200–201. You may reproduce these cards for use in the classroom. As you discover effective management techniques, highlight them and share them with parents.

2. Share your concerns with the parents and document your observations with work samples, anecdotal information, videotape, testing data, and so on.

3. Invite parents to observe their child in the classroom or therapy session. This is particularly advisable if the child has not been diagnosed. Because children with ADHD have particular difficulty in group situations, parents may be unaware of the child's behavior.

4. If the child is being served by a multidisciplinary team, work with the team to develop effective treatment strategies.

5. If the child is on medication, complete a checklist when requested. Learn about possible side effects, and be alert for them. Because many children take medication during school hours, side effects may not be evident to parents.

6. Recognize that medication aids only with attention and impulsivity. It does not eliminate other behaviors, and it is far from being an instant cure. A child who fidgets may continue to do so under medication.

7. Involve the school nurse or any available on-site health professional. Make sure the parents are introduced to the school nurse and know how to contact him or her.

8. Actively communicate with parents, using a traveling notebook when direct communication is not possible. Share positive statements about the child, and encourage parents to share interventions they are using at home.

9. Provide encouragement to the parents and others working with the child. Communicate the need to work together as a team.

10. Provide a list of community resources (parent support groups, classes, family enrichment activities, and so on). See page 178 for a list of national resources.

11. Keep a bibliography of current articles, pamphlets, and books to share with parents seeking further information. See pages 177–179 for a "starter" bibliography.

12. Educate yourself about current interventions, strategies, resources, and medications.

13. Be good to yourself! You are invaluable in the child's life. Each intervention you employ is propelling the child toward success!

Many parents of children with attention deficit feel anxious about the child's first day in preschool. Research has indicated that notes home do make a difference. The personal note is a way to open the door to communication the first day. See figure 3, the sample One-Minute Memo. Use the blank forms on pages 202–203 as a guide for providing a daily report home.

The teacher or therapist can also help parents by providing a list of books that parents can read to children about difficulties with attentional concerns. See page 179 for a listing of a variety of such books.

All of these suggestions are designed to develop a working partnership between the professionals and the parents to meet both the child's and the family's needs. Working with children with attentional concerns presents many challenges each day, but children with ADHD also can be the most rewarding children in a home or classroom. The teacher's or caregiver's responsibility is to ensure that every child feels some success in the experiences of the day. We do this by providing an appropriate amount of support, direction, and independence so that every child can participate at an optimal level.

FIGURE 3
Sample One-Minute Memo

One-Minute Memo

First Day Jitters?
We had them too!
Here are some things to share with you!

Child's name   Lindsay

Liked to play with   blocks

Needed help with   putting toys away

Told us   she has a black cat

Ask your child to tell you about   what happened to Mr. Jingles, the puppet

Tomorrow   we make cookies!

Signed   Mrs. Jones

Parent Resources

Books

Fowler, M. *Maybe You Know My Kid*. New York: Birch Lane Press, 1992.

Goldstein S., and M. Goldstein. *A Parent's Guide: Attention Deficit-Hyperactivity Disorder in Children*. Salt Lake City: Neurology, Learning, and Behavior Center, 1989.

Heart, L. *The Winning Family*. Oakland, CA: Lifeskills Press, 1989.

Ingersol, E. *The Hyperactive Child*. New York: Doubleday, 1988.

Levine, M. *All Kinds of Minds*. Cambridge, MA: Educators Publishing Service, 1993.

Moss, R., and H. Dunlap. *Why Johnny Can't Concentrate*. New York: Bantam, 1990.

Turecki, S., and L. Toner. *The Difficult Child*. New York: Bantam, 1985.

Videotapes

Barkley, R. *ADHD: What Do We Know?* New York: Guilford, 1993.

_____. *ADHD: What Can We Do?* New York: Guilford, 1993.

Goldstein, S. *Why Won't My Child Pay Attention?* Salt Lake City: Neurology, Learning, and Behavior Center, 1989.

Gordon, M. *Jumping Johnny, Get Back to Work*. DeWitt, NY: GSI, 1993

Phelam, T. *Attention Deficit/Hyperactivity Disorder*. Glen Ellyn, IL: Child Management, 1992.

_____. *One-Two-Three Magic: Training Your Preschooler and Preteen to Do What You Want Them to Do*. Glen Ellyn, IL: Child Management, 1992.

National Newsletters

Challenge, A Newsletter on ADHD
P.O. Box 2001
W. Newbury, MA 01985
(508) 462-0495

CHADDER, Biannual publication of
Children and Adults with Attention
Deficit Disorder (CH.A.A.D.)
499 NW 70th Ave., Suite 102
Plantation, FL 33317
(305) 792-8944

Attention, Biannual publication of Children
and Adults with Attention Deficit
Disorder (CH.A.A.D.)
499 NW 70th Ave., Suite 102
Plantation, FL 33317
(305) 792-8944

Special Parent/Special Child
Lindell Press
P.O. Box 462
South Salem, NY 10590
(914) 763-5568

Add-Vance, a publication of Attention
Deficit Disorder Association
8091 South Ireland Way
Aurora, CO 80016
(303) 690-7548

National Organizations

*American Academy of Child and
Adolescent Psychiatry*
3615 Wisconsin Avenue, NW
Washington, D.C. 20016
(202) 966-7300

American Academy of Pediatrics
P.O. Box 927
141 Northwest Point Blvd.
Elk Grove Village, IL 63009
(312) 981-7935

*American Association of Children's
Residential Centers*
440 First Street, N.W., Suite 310
Washington D.C. 20001
(202) 638-1604

American Family Therapy Association
2550 M Street, N.W., Suite 275
Washington, D.C. 20037

American Psychological Association
1200 17th Street, N.W.
Washington, D.C. 20036
(202) 955-7618

American School Counselor Association
5999 Stevenson Avenue
Alexandria, VA 22304
(703) 823-9800

American School Health Association
P.O. Box 708
Kent, OH 44240

Association of Educational Therapists
P.O. Box 946
Woodland Hills, CA 91365
(818) 788-3850

*Children and Adults with Attention Deficit
Disorder (CH.A.D.D.)*
499 N.W. 70th Avenue, Suite 102
Plantation, FL 33317
(305) 792-8944
Home-page address: www.chadd.org

Council for Exceptional Children
1920 Association Drive
Reston, VA 22091
(703) 620-3660

*Foundation for Children with Learning
Disabilities*
99 Park Ave.
New York, NY 10016
(212) 687-7211

Learning Disabilities Association
4156 Library Road
Pittsburgh, PA 15234
(412) 341-1515

*National Association for the Education
of Young Children*
1834 Connecticut Ave., N.W.
Washington D.C., 20009-5786
(800) 424-2460

*National Information Center for
Handicapped Children and Youth*
P.O. Box 1492
Washington, D.C. 20013
(703) 893-6061

Books to Read to Children

Galvin, M. *Otto Learns About His Medicine: A Story About Medication for Hyperactive Children.* New York: Imagination Press, 1988.

Gordon, M. *Jumping Johnny, Get Back to Work.* DeWitt, NY: GSI Publications, 1991.

_____. *Juanito Saltarin: A Tu Tarbajo de Nuevo!* DeWitt, NY: GSI Publications, 1995.

Moss, D. *Shelley, The Hyperactive Turtle.* Kensington, MD: Woodbine House, 1989.

Nadeau, K., and E. Dixson. *Learning to Slow Down and Pay Attention.* New York: Brunner-Mazel, 1997. (Ages 6-10)

Quinn, P. *Putting on the Brakes.* New York: Brunner-Mazel, 1994.

Shapiro, L. *Sometimes I Drive My Mom Crazy, But I Know She's Crazy About Me.* King of Prussia, PA: The Center for Applied Psychology, 1993.

Internet

CH.A.D.D. Home-page address: www.chadd.org

For servers who use American Online: Attention Deficit Disorder Support is listed under key word PEN (Positive Empowerment Network). Chat Group, Resource Information, and other resources on Attention Deficit Disorder are available at this key word.

Attention Deficit Disorder

What is Attention Deficit Disorder (ADD or AD/HD)?
Attention deficit disorder is a term used to describe children who are inattentive, impulsive, and frequently very active. This observed hyperactivity is higher than we would expect from same-age children.

Who can diagnose ADD (AD/HD)?
Your family physician or pediatrician can help you get started. You may be referred by your doctor to a psychologist or diagnostic specialist who can help you identify your child's specific needs.

What are the diagnostic criteria for ADD (AD/HD)?
For the diagnosis to be made, it is necessary for six or more of the following symptoms to be present for at least six months. These symptoms should be present from preschool on. They should be seen both at home and in school, to be sure that these behaviors are not just a reaction to school.

Criteria for Attention Deficit/Hyperactivity Disorder*
A. Either 1 or 2.
1. Six (or more) of the following symptoms of inattention have persisted for at least six months to a degree that is maladaptive and inconsistent with developmental level:

   ### Inattention
   a. Often fails to give close attention to details or makes careless mistakes in schoolwork, work, or other activities.
   b. Often has difficulties sustaining attention in tasks or play activities.
   c. Often does not seem to listen when spoken to directly.
   d. Often does not follow through on instructions and fails to finish school-work, chores, or duties in the workplace (not due to oppositional behavior or failure to understand instructions).
   e. Often has difficulty organizing tasks and activities.
   f. Often avoids, dislikes, or is reluctant to engage in tasks that require sustained mental effort (such as schoolwork or homework).
   g. Often loses things necessary for tasks or activities (for example, school assignments, pencils, books, or tools).
   h. Is often easily distracted by extraneous stimuli.
   i. Is often forgetful in daily activities.

2. Six (or more) of the following symptoms of hyperactivity-impulsivity have persisted for at least six months to a degree that is maladaptive and inconsistent with developmental level:

(continued)

***FACT SHEET** (continued)*

Hyperactivity
a. Often fidgets with hands or feet or squirms in seat.
b. Often leaves seat in classroom or in other situations in which remaining seated is expected.
c. Often runs about or climbs excessively in situations in which it is inappropriate. (In adolescents or adults, may be limited to subjective feelings of restlessness.)
d. Often has difficulty playing or engaging in leisure activities quietly.
e. Is often "on the go" or often acts as if "driven by a motor."
f. Often talks excessively.

Impulsivity
g. Often blurts out answers before questions have been completed.
h. Often has difficulty awaiting turn.
i. Often interrupts or intrudes on others (for example, butts into conversations or games).

B. Some hyperactive-impulsive or inattentive symptoms that caused impairment were present before the age of seven.

C. Some impairment from the symptoms is present in two or more situations (for example, at school, at work, or at home).

D. There must be clear evidence of clinically significant impairment in social, academic, or occupational functioning.

E. The symptoms do not occur exclusively during the course of pervasive developmental disorder, schizophrenias or other psychotic disorders, and are not better accounted for by another mental disorder (for example, mood disorder, anxiety disorder, dissociative disorder, or personality disorder).

*Reprinted with permission from the *Diagnostic and Statistical Manual of Mental Disorders,* Fourth Edition. Copyright 1994 American Psychiatric Association.

What are the possible causes of ADD (ADHD)?
ADHD appears to be the result of multiple genetic, prenatal, or physical factors. It seems to exist in family history (that is, it may be hereditary). More boys than girls appear to have ADD (AD/HD). It may also be the factor if the mother used or abused alcohol or drugs during pregnancy.

What are educational accommodations?
Accommodations are strategies and techniques that teachers can use to help students succeed in the classroom at their own level. Some of these techniques include preferential seating, less written work, more time to copy work from board to paper; smaller chunks of required work; and peer tutoring. AD/HD students will benefit when teachers can adapt the class work to fit what they can do.

What are some medical options?
All youngsters with ADD should be referred to a physician for a physical examination. Many children benefit from psychostimulant medication, social modeling, counseling, and behavior modification.

Desorden de Déficit de Atención

¿Que es el desorden de déficit de atención (DDA)?
Desorden de déficit de atención es el término que se usa para describir a niños que son inatentos, impulsivos y, frecuentemente, extremadamente activos. Esta hiperactividad aparente es más marcada en estos niños que en otros niños de la misma edad.

¿Quién puede hacer el diagnostico de DDA?
Su medico o su pediatra le pueden ayudar. Es posible que su medico le envíe a un psicólogo o a un especialista en la diagnostica quien le pueda ayudar a identificar los requerimientos especiales de su hijo.

¿Cuáles son los criterios para el diagnostico de DDA?
La lista que sigue (del *Manual diagnostico y estadistico de desordenes mentales* del American Psychiatric Association) contiene símptomas o comportamientos que pueden estar presentes en los niños con desórdenes de atención. La persona que hace el diagnostico debe asegurar que el niño ha demostrado seis o más de estos símptomas por no menos de seis meses. Estos comportamientos deben ser evidentes tanto en casa como en la escuela.

Criteria for Attention Deficit/Hyperactivity Disorder*
A. Either 1 or 2.
  1. Six (or more) of the following symptoms of inattention have persisted for at least six months to a degree that is maladaptive and inconsistent with developmental level:
  Inattention
      a. Often fails to give close attention to details or makes careless mistakes in schoolwork, work, or other activities.
      b. Often has difficulties sustaining attention in tasks or play activities.
      c. Often does not seem to listen when spoken to directly.
      d. Often does not follow through on instructions and fails to finish school-work, chores, or duties in the workplace (not due to oppositional behavior or failure to understand instructions).
      e. Often has difficulty organizing tasks and activities.
      f. Often avoids, dislikes, or is reluctant to engage in tasks that require sustained mental effort (such as schoolwork or homework).
      g. Often loses things necessary for tasks or activities (for example, school assignments, pencils, books, or tools).
      h. Is often easily distracted by extraneous stimuli.
      i. Is often forgetful in daily activities.
  2. Six (or more) of the following symptoms of hyperactivity-impulsivity have persisted for at least six months to a degree that is maladaptive and inconsistent with developmental level:

(continua)

Hyperactivity

a. Often fidgets with hands or feet or squirms in seat.

b. Often leaves seat in classroom or in other situations in which remaining seated is expected.

c. Often runs about or climbs excessively in situations in which it is inappropriate. (In adolescents or adults, may be limited to subjective feelings of restlessness.)

d. Often has difficulty playing or engaging in leisure activities quietly.

e. Is often "on the go" or often acts as if "driven by a motor."

f. Often talks excessively.

Impulsivity

g. Often blurts out answers before questions have been completed.

h. Often has difficulty awaiting turn.

i. Often interrupts or intrudes on others (for example, butts into conversations or games).

B. Some hyperactive-impulsive or inattentive symptoms that caused impairment were present before the age of seven.

C. Some impairment from the symptoms is present in two or more situations (for example, at school, at work, or at home).

D. There must be clear evidence of clinically significant impairment in social, academic, or occupational functioning.

E. The symptoms do not occur exclusively during the course of pervasive developmental disorder, schizophrenias or other psychotic disorders, and are not better accounted for by another mental disorder (for example, mood disorder, anxiety disorder, dissociative disorder, or personality disorder).

*Reprinted with permission from the *Diagnostic and Statistical Manual of Mental Disorders,* Fourth Edition. Copyright 1994 American Psychiatric Association.

¿Cuáles pueden ser las causas de DDA?

DDA parece ser el resultado de varios factores, incluso geneticos, prenatales y físicos. Parece formar parte de la historia medica familiar (en otras palabras, puede ser hereditario). Incluso, DDA se ve más en niños que en niñas. Si la madre abusó de bebidas alcoholicas o drogas durante el embarazo, también puede tener algo que ver.

¿Qué son acomodaciones escolares?

Acomodaciones son estrategias y técnicas que los maestros pueden usar para ayudar a sus estudiantes a ser exitosos en el salón de clases a su propio nivel. Algunas de estas técnicas incluyen: asiento preferencial, menos trabajo por escrito, más tiempo para copiar el trabajo del pisarón al papel, trozos más pequeños de tarea, y tutela de los compañeros. Los estudiantes con DDA se benefician cuando los maestros pueden adaptar el trabajo hecho en clase a sus habilidades.

¿Cuáles son algunas opciones médicas?

Todos los chicos que tienen DDA deben ser examinados por un médico. Para muchos niños pueden ser útiles los medicamentos psicoestimulantes, la pragmática, la psicoterapia, y la modificación del comportamiento.

Common Problems of Children with Attention Disorders

Trait	Manifestations
Poor selective attention	Tends to focus on unimportant parts of a job. Can't seem to "tune out" distractions. Hates detail.
Cognitive fatigue	Yawns frequently. Tires quickly when required to sit still and do a structured task, such as schoolwork. Gives up easily on tasks.
Insatiable	Wants everything "right now." Has difficulty waiting for a reward or special event. Tends to want things all the time. Is always thinking ahead about the end result. Does not plan step by step, but jumps ahead to the end result.
Impulsive	Acts too quickly, without planning.
Inconsistent performance	"Some days they can; some days they can't." Your child may do well on a test one day, then fail one the next day. Some days the child seems to pay attention to you; other days, forget it!
Inappropriate activity	Is (sometimes) overactive. Sometimes has difficulty paying attention while doing something.
Poor self-monitoring	"She doesn't seem to think about what she's doing." Does not check over assignments for errors. Sometimes does not try to control behavior.
Poor memory	Has difficulty remembering specific facts and putting them together. Is likely to be behind in school, especially at the high school level.
Motor dysfunctions	Has problems with small hand and eye movements (called fine motor skills). Has difficulty with tasks such as writing that require putting several movements together.

Adapted with permission from Levine, M., and N. Jordan. Learning Disorders: The Neurodevelopmental Underpinnings. *Contemporary Pediatrics* 4(8):20. Copyright © (1987) by Medical Economics Publishing, Inc., Montvale, NJ.

Problemas Comunes de los Niños con Déficit de Atención

Manifestación de las características

Pobre atención selectiva

Acostumbra fijarse sobre las partes poco importantes de un trabajo. Le falta la habilidad de no hacer caso a las distracciones. Odia los detalles.

Fatiga cognitiva

Bosteza frecuentemente. Se cansa rápidamente cuando tiene que quedarse quieto y hacer un trabajo detallado como las tareas escolares. Se da por vencido fácilmente.

Insaciable

Quiere todo "ahora." Le es difícil aguardar algun premio o evento especial. Quiere cosas todo el tiempo. Siempre piensa en el resultado final. No planea paso a paso, sino que "salta" al resultado final.

Impulsivo

Actua demasiado rápido, sin planear lo que va a hacer.

Desempeño desigual

Algunos días puede, otros días no. Su niño puede sacarse una buena calificación en una prueba un día, y sacarse un cero el otro. Algunos días el niño parece poner atención, y otros diás, ¡olvídelo!

Actividad no apropiada

A veces es demasiado activo. A veces tiene dificultad para poner atención cuando está tratando de hacer algo.

Pobre auto-dirección

"Parece que no piensa en lo que hace." No revisa sus tareas para corregir errores. A veces no trata de controlar su comportamiento.

Mala memoria

Tiene dificultad para recordar hechos específicos y entrelazarlos. Probablemente se retrasa en la escuela, especialmente en la secundaria.

Mal funcionamiento motorico

Tiene problemas con movimientos pequeños de la mano y los ojos (habilidades motóricas, *fine motor skills*). Tiene dificultades con habilidades tales como escribir, que requieren el agrupamiento de varios movimientos.

Adapted with permission from Levine, M., and N. Jordan. Learning Disorders: The Neurodevelopmental Underpinnings. *Contemporary Pediatrics* 4(8):20. Copyright © (1987) by Medical Economics Publishing, Inc., Montvale, NJ.

Coping with Attention Deficit Disorder

1. Let your child know that you love him or her no matter what. Your child is special, and both of you will make mistakes as you grow together.

2. Your child's problems are *not* your fault. Attention deficit disorder is not caused by bad parenting or something you did.

3. Learn all you can about ADD. Read articles, talk to professionals and other parents, and attend conferences and workshops.

4. You know your child better than anyone, and what you've learned can help others. Share things that have worked at home with your child's teachers and therapists.

5. You are your child's advocate. Your child has a right to a "free and appropriate public education" according to Public Law 94-142 and Section 504 of the Rehabilitation Act. Learn about these laws, and understand the guarantees that they offer to your child.

6. Show that you believe in your child's abilities. Focus on your child's strengths, and endorse each attempt to succeed. Many children with ADD feel like failures and give up before they have a chance to succeed.

7. Be consistent. Establish basic rules when your child is young, and keep those rules into the teenage years.

8. Establish a routine in your home, because your child won't take surprises and changes well. As much as possible, arrange a routine for eating snacks and meals and going to bed at the same time every day.

9. Prepare your child for any change in the routine. Give the child plenty of notice about the change, and talk about what will be happening. ("We're going to go to the grocery store together. You will sit in the cart. I need you to hold the list. If you do a good job, you can pick out your own fruit.")

10. Use lists to help your child manage chores at home. Sit down with the child and make a list of things to be done. Keep the list short. Write down only things that have to be done right away. (Remember that your child isn't good at planning and remembering things for very long.) If your child can't read yet, use simple drawings or symbols to symbolize the jobs. Have the child cross each task off the list when it is completed. Let your child know that there will be a reward for completing the list.

(continued)

11. Build self-discipline and a sense of responsibility. Assign chores that are the same as any other child. Children with ADD don't do well when they have to do the same thing over and over; so make a "job jar" full of "chore cards" on which you list jobs that need to be done. Let your child choose a card on a regular basis. Younger children can help by dusting, folding laundry, or feeding a pet. Older children might have jobs ranging from household repairs to meal preparation.

12. Your child might get "stuck" talking about one thing. When this happens, offer a diversion to redirect the child's attention.

13. Children with ADD have a hard time keeping their thoughts in order. If your child starts to ramble when telling you about something, ask the four questions: What? Where? When? Why?

14. Keep directions short and sweet. Some active children will be able to follow only one simple direction at a time.

15. Give your child lots of well-marked storage space to organize belongings. Crates are a good choice, especially if you can get different colors. On the outside, glue a picture of what's to go inside (for example, a blue box with a picture of shoes on the front, and a yellow box with a picture of socks).

16. Place drawers, shelves, and hooks where the child can see and reach them. Then your child can learn to do more things without help.

17. Talk to professionals about good ways to handle your child's behavior.

18. Work together with other important people in the child's life to provide a positive and united front.

Hacer Frente al Déficit de Atención

1. Hágale saber a su niño que lo quiere a pesar de todo. Su hijo es especial, y tanto usted como él se equivocarán de vez en cuando al crecer juntos.

2. Los problemas que tiene su hijo ¡no son culpa de usted! El déficit de la atención no surge a causa de ser malos padres o de algo que usted hizo.

3. Aprenda todo lo que pueda sobre déficit de atención. Lea artículos, hable con profesionales y otros padres, y asista a conferencias.

4. Usted conoce a su hijo mejor que nadie. Lo que ha aprendido puede ayudar a los demás. Comparta con los maestros y terapeutas de su hijo lo que usted ha hecho en casa.

5. Usted es el defensór de su hijo. Su hijo tiene el deber a una "educación apropiada grátis" según la Ley Publica 94-142 y la Sección 504 del Acto de Rehabilitación. Familiarízese con estas leyes, y con las garantías que le ofrecen a su hijo.

6. Enséñele a su hijo que usted cree en él y en sus habilidades. Fíjese sobre lo que su niño hace bien, y fomente cada atento para lograr éxito. Muchos niños con déficit de atención se sienten como fracasos y se dan por vencidos antes de tener la oportunidad para lograr ser exitosos.

7. Sea consistente. Establezca reglas cuando su niño es pequeño y no las olvide cuando su niño llega a ser adolescente.

8. Establezca una rutina diaria en casa, porque su hijo no tolera bien los cambios y las sorpresas. En cuanto le es posible, fije la hora de la cena y la hora de acostarse.

9. Prepare a su hijo antes de cambiar la rutina. Advierta al niño de cualquier cambio y hable con él acerca de lo que va a suceder. (ej. "Vamos a la tienda juntos. Tú te vas a sentar en el carrito. Necesito que tú detengas la lista. Si lo haces bien, puedes escojer la fruta que quieras.")

10. Use listas para las tareas caseras. Siéntase con su hijo y haga una lista de los quehaceres. La lista debe ser corta. Apunte solamente lo que se tiene que hacer ahora. (Recuerde que su hijo no planea bien, y que tiene corta memoria.) Si su hijo todavia no sabe leer, use dibujos sencillos u otros símbolos para representar las varias tareas. Pídale al niño que tache cada tarea en cuanta la acabe. Recuerdele que ganará un premio si completa cada tarea en la lista.

(continua)

11. Fomente la auto-disciplina y un sentido de responsabilidad. Asigne tareas al igual que a otros niños. Niños con déficit de atención no se comportan bien cuando tienen que hacer tareas muy repetitivas; anote varias tareas en unas tarjetas y guárdelas en un frasco. Deje que su niño escoja la tarjeta que quiera. Los niños más chicos pueden sacudir, guardar ropa, o darle de comer al perro. Niños mayores pueden hacer reparos sencillos o preparar la comida.

12. Es posible que su hijo se "atore" hablando sobre un tema. Si esto sucede, ofrezca alguna diversion para redijir su atención.

13. Niños con déficit de atención tienen problemas para ordenar sus pensamientos. Si su hijo empieza a dar vueltas mientras le esta hablando de algo, pregúntele las siguientes cuatro preguntas: ¿Que? ¿Donde? ¿Cuando? y ¿Por qué?

14. De instrucciones cortas y sencillas. Algunos niños muy activos nada más pueden seguir una instrucción a la vez.

15. Aparte mucho lugar para que su hijo guarde sus cosas. Las cajas o cajones de plástico son muy útiles, especialmente si son de varios colores. Por afuera, fije un dibujo de lo que va a ir adentro (ej., un cajón azul con un dibujo de zapatos, y un cajón amarillo con un dibujo de calcetines.

16. Coloque cajones, estantes y ganchos donde el niño las pueda alcanzar. Asi su niño podrá hacer más cosas por si mismo.

17. Hable con profesionales sobre como manejar el comportamiento de su hijo.

18. Reúnase con otras gentes que le importan a su hijo y traten juntos de presentar una frente unida y positiva para con su hijo.

Coping with Your Child's Behavior

1. "Catch" your child being good, and give a reward right away. Reward behaviors you want to see again.

2. With your actions and words, let your child see how proud you are of him or her. Show pleasure in your child's progress toward learning self-control.

3. Don't haggle or argue about small things. Once you have made a decision and shared it with your child, stick with it. For example, don't let your child argue with you about watching one more television show or staying up past bedtime.

4. Accept that your child will be absent-minded. It may seem that you are always reminding your child about something, but try not to get annoyed and say things like, "If I have to tell you one more time!" Repeat directions as if you were telling the child for the first time. Try to state the directions in a different way, and try to use things your child can see and hear as reminders.

5. Make directions brief. First, get your child's attention. Then slowly state what to do, using simple words and short sentences. Start with one direction, and gradually give longer directions as your child is able to remember them. Keep your voice calm, and avoid sounding sarcastic or annoyed. Ask your child to repeat what you said. (Not only does this help your child remember, but you can also make sure you understood each other.) Reward the child immediately with verbal or physical praise.

6. Make rules specific. State briefly and precisely what you expect (for example, "Take turns talking"; "Put your feet on the floor"). Avoid vague rules, such as, "Be nice to your sister."

7. Post rules in your home. Decide as a family what the rules are, and post them where they can be easily seen. For example, you might post these dinnertime rules on the refrigerator:
   1. Use your fork to eat.
   2. Chew with your mouth closed.
   3. Ask for permission to leave the table before getting up.

8. If you must punish the child, make it clear that the punishment is for breaking a rule, not because you are "being mean."

9. Any rule at home also should be a rule in a public place. The child needs to expect the same consequence.

(continued)

10. Help your child learn to make good choices and to think before acting. When you can, give the child a chance to make choices. Give two clear choices, both of which you will accept.

    Try this:
    > Parent: We are going to visit Grandma. You may wear your blue shirt or your red one. Which one do you choose?

    Not this:
    > Parent: What are you going to wear to Grandma's?
    > Child: My cowboy suit.
    > Parent: Oh, no, you won't!

11. Respond immediately to a behavior, whether it's good or bad. Show your child that behaviors have immediate consequences.

12. Reward the child for a particular behavior, not for generally "being good." Make sure the child knows exactly what the reward is for. This way, your child will learn, "This is a good thing I can do by myself, without Mom or Dad telling me."

    Try this:
    > Parent: You were really thinking when you shut off that water so quickly.

    Not this:
    > Parent: You are the smartest kid on earth.

13. Be tolerant, and ignore some behaviors. Some active children develop habits such as tapping their fingers or humming. By not reacting, you are not rewarding the behavior.

Hacer Frente al Comportamiento de su Hijo

1. "Sorpendalo" cuando se está portando bien, y dele un premio inmediatamente. Premie comportamiento que usted quiere ver de nuevo.

2. A traves de sus acciones y sus palabras, deje que su hijo sepa que orgulloso se siente de él. Deje que su niño vea que le da a usted mucho placer cuando ve que su hijo esta avanzando en el camino hacia el control de si mismo.

3. No discuta con su niño los asuntos de poca importancia. Cuando ha hecho usted una decisión, y se la ha dicho a su hijo, ¡no la cambie! Por ejemplo, no deje que su niño discuta con usted si puede ver un programa más de television, o si se tiene que ir a la cama.

4. Acepte que su niño tiene mala memoria. A veces parece que siempre le tiene que recordar algo, pero trate de no enojarse y decir cosas como, "¡Si te lo tengo que decir una vez más….!" Repita las direcciones como si se las fuera diciendo por primera vez. Trate de repetir las direcciones de una manera distinta, y trate de usar cosas que su hijo puede ver y oir como recordatorios.

5. Haga sus direcciones breves. Primero, capte la atención de su hijo. Luego, usando palabras sencillas y oraciones cortas, lentamente dígale lo que quiere usted que haga. Empiece con una dirección y agregue direcciones gradualmente, a la vez que su hijo las pueda recordar. Quédese calmado, e intente no sonar enojado o sarcastico. Pídale a su niño que le repita lo que le dijo. (Esto no solo ayuda que recuerde su hijo lo que usted le ha dicho; ademas puede asegurarse usted que se han entendido.) Premie al niño inmediatamente con palabras o cariños.

6. Haga reglas específicas. Diga exactamente lo que quiere que su niño haga (ej., "Espera que termine de hablar"; "Pon tus pies en el piso"). Evite reglas indefinidas, tales como, "Portate bien con tu hermana."

7. Fije la lista de reglas. Decídanse como familia cuales van a ser las reglas, y péguelas donde todos las pueden ver. Por ejemplo, pueden fijar al refrigerador las siguientes reglas sobre el comportamiento a la hora de la cena:
   1. Usa tu teneder
   2. Mastica con la boca cerrada
   3. Pide permiso antes de retirarte de la mesa

8. Si tiene que castigar al niño, asegúrele que el castigo es porque no siguió las reglas, no porque es usted "una persona mala."

9. Cualquier regla en casa también se aplica a sitios públicos. El niño debe esperar las mismas consecuencias.

(continua)

10. Ayude a sus niño a hacer buenas decisiones y a pensar antes de actuar. Cuando sea posible, deje que su niño haga decisiones por si mismo. Presente dos opciones aceptables.

    Diga esto:
    Padre: Vamos a visitar a abuelita. Puedes usar tu camisa azul o la verde. ¿Cual escojes?

    NO esto:
    Padre: ¿Que te vas a poner para ir a casa de abuelita?
    Niño: Mi traje de vaquero.
    Padre: ¡A, no! ¡Ni lo pienses!

11. Responda por inmediato a cualquier comportamiento, sea bueno o malo. Enséñele a su hijo que los comportamientos tienen consecuencias inmediatas.

12. Premie al niño por un comportamiento en particular, no solamente por "portarse bien." Asegurese que el niño sabe exactamente porqué le dió un premio. De esta manera, su niño aprenderá que: "Esto es algo bueno que puedo hacer solito, sin que Mamá o Papá me lo tenga que decir."

    Diga esto:
    Padre: De veras que hiciste bien cuando apagaste el agua tan rápido.

    NO esto:
    Padre: ¡Eres el niño mas listo del mundo!

13. Sea tolerante, y no haga caso a algunos comportamientos. Algunos niños muy activos desarollan costumbres como jugar con los dedos o hacer zumbidos. Si usted no le hace caso, no esta fomentando ese comportamiento.

Taking Your Child to Public Places

1. Think ahead to social situations that may be difficult. Will your child get bored or cause difficulty?

2. Before going into the situation:
   - Review your standing rules.
   - Agree with your child on a reward for behaving well.
   - Clearly state a consequence for noncompliance.

3. Have your child restate the rule, consequence, and reward to make sure the child understands and remembers.

4. Remind your child about the reward in a positive way while you are in the situation. Don't threaten the child.
   Try this:
     "If you remember to . . ., you'll get to . . ."
   Not this:
     "If you don't shape up right now, you won't get to . . . ."

5. Give the reward immediately on leaving the public place.

Example:

- *Anticipate.* You have to take your child grocery shopping with you. You know your child has difficulty waiting in line and grabs candy by the cash register.

- *Review the rule.* "When we are in line, keep your hands to yourself. I'd like you to hold my purse while I pay."

- *Determine a reward.* "You wanted to go to the duck pond. If you keep your hands to yourself, we'll stop by the duck pond and feed the ducks."

- *Review a consequence.* "If you take any candy, we won't see the ducks."

- *Have the child restate the rule and the reward.* "Hands to myself. I can feed the ducks if I keep my hands to myself."

- *Positively state the reward as you shop.* "It's great to know we will be feeding the ducks! Do you want to take bread or corn?"

- *Reward your child immediately.* Drive from the grocery store straight to the duck pond. State, "When you follow the rules, nice things happen."

(*continued*)

6. If your child appears to be forgetting the rule, call attention to something else, and positively state the reward again.

    Try this:

    "Oh, look! There's a picture of a duck on that box. I wonder if we will see a duck like that?"

    Not this:

    "You better behave, or no ducks for you."

7. Avoid using the word *don't*. State something positive while you direct your child toward what you expect.

    Try this:

    "I want to see your hands on the table."

    Not this:

    "Don't touch that plant!"

8. Keep your child involved. If your child will have to wait quietly, bring along something special to play with. Keep a box of small toys and books in your car just for this purpose.

9. Try to offer a balance between structured and unstructured activities. Remember, your child can do a formal "sit-down" activity for only a short time.

10. Learn to see trouble coming. When you see your child starting to lose control in a situation, step in right away. Offer a diversion that will help your child gain control. Do not encourage the overactive behavior to continue.

11. Take care of yourself! At times, you may need to remove yourself from a difficult situation to cool off. Is there a friend or neighbor nearby whom you can call on short notice to take care of your child, even for only ten minutes? Remind yourself of everything you are doing and the progress your child is making. Your efforts *will* make a difference!

Cuando Lleva a Su Niño Fuera de Casa

1. De antemano, determine si alguna situación social va a ser difícil para su hijo. ¿Se va a aburrir el niño o va a causar problemas?

2. Antes de entrar en la situación

    • Haga un repaso de las reglas

    • Arreglense usted y su hijo sobre cual premio se va a ganar si se porta bien

    • Dígale a su hijo claramente cuáles van a ser las consecuencias si no se porta bien

3. Haga que su niño le repita las reglas, las consecuencias y el premio para asegurarse que entendió y recordó lo que usted le acaba de decir.

4. Recuérdele a su hijo del premio mientras estén en la situación. No le de advertencias.

    Diga esto:

    "Si te acuerdas de. . ., vas a poder . . ."

    NO esto:

    "Si no te portas bien ahorita, no te voy a dejar. . ."

5. Dele su premio inmediatamente despues de salir del sitio o de la situación.

Ejemplo:

• *Anticipe.* Tiene que llevarse a su hijo do compras. Sabe usted que a su hijo le cuesta trabajo esperar en fila y que agarra los dulces de los estantes junto a la caja.

• *Revise la regla.* "Cuando estamos en fila, no toques nada. Quiero que me detengas la bolsa mientras le pago a la cajera."

• *Determine un premio.* "Querias ir a darle de comer a los patos. Si no tocas nada, te llevo a ver a los patitos."

• *Repase las consecuencias.* "Si agarras un dulce, no vamos a ver a los patos."

• *Pídale al niño que le repita el premio mientras usted hace sus compras.* "No tocar nada. Puedo darle de comer a los patos si no toco nada."

• *Repita usted el premio de manera positiva mientras hace las compras.* "¡Que bueno que les vamos a dar a comer a los patos! ¿Quieres llevarles pan o maíz?"

• *Premie a su hijo inmediatamente.* Conduzca de la tienda directamente al lago. Diga, "Cuando sigues las reglas, pasan cosas bonitas."

(continua)

6. Si su hijo parece estar olvidando la regla, llámele la atencion a otra cosa, y repita el premio de manera positiva otra vez.

    Diga esto:

    > "¡Mira! Hay un dibujo de un pato en esta caja. A ver si vemos un pato como ese."

    NO esto:

    > "Más te vale que te portes bien, o no vas a ver ni un solo pato."

7. Evite usar la palabra *No.* Trate de decir algo positivo al dirijir a su niño hacia lo que espera usted que haga.

    Diga esto:

    > "Quiero ver tus manos sobre la mesa."

    NO esto:

    > "¡No toques esa planta!"

8. Mantenga el interés de su hijo. Si su niño va a tener que esperarse quieto, traiga un juguete especial. Guarde dentro de su coche una caja llena de libros y juguetes pequeños sólo para estas ocasiones.

9. Trate de balancear las actividades estructuradas con las actividades libres. Recuerde, su hijo no puede prestar atención a una sola actividad por mucho tiempo.

10. Aprenda a anticipar los problems. Cuando ve que su niño ya no se puede controlar en alguna situacion, intervengase inmediatamente. Ofrezca alguna diversión que le ayudará a su niño controlarse de nuevo. No fomente el comportamiento demasiado activo.

11. ¡Cuídese! A veces tendrá que retirarse de una situacion dificil para calmarse. ¿Le puede pedir a algún amigo o vecino cercano que le cuide a su hijo por un rato, aunque sea por diez minutos? Siga recordándose de todo lo que está haciendo y de como está avanzando su hijo. ¡Sus esfuerzos *sí* valen la pena!

Keeping Your Child Safe

Children with ADD experience more accidental poisonings and trips to the emergency room than do other children. There are several reasons why your child may be accident prone: Your child is impulsive and may do such things as running out into the street without looking. Your child seems to have no fear of jumping off the porch roof on a dare. The child may eat or drink something poisonous. You need to be aware of what your child is up to at all times. Take steps to make your house and yard safe and childproof.

1. Watch closely when your child is playing outside. Keep glass, rocks, and other sharp items away from where your child plays. Secure trash bins. Ask neighbors to watch for your child as well.

2. Lock medicines, cleaning supplies, and other poisons where even the most determined child can't get them.

3. Cover all electrical outlets.

4. Put large, colorful stickers on sliding glass doors.

5. If you have a pool, make sure it is well fenced. Never leave your child unattended in the pool area.

6. Protect items that you value. Put glass figurines, china, and jewelry out of reach.

7. Place locked screens on all windows to prevent falls.

8. Firmly tie the cords of blinds or drapes. Do not allow them to hang loose.

9. Store electrical appliances, knives, and tools in a locked cupboard away from areas the child frequents.

10. Secure loose cords and wires so your child can't trip on them.

11. Select toys that stand up to heavy use.

12. Compliment your child for playing safely. ("Well done! You know the right way to use the scissors!") Draw attention to other children who are playing safely.

Prevenir los Accidentes

Los niños con déficit de atención se envenenan por accidente y necesitan ir a la sala de emergencias con más frecuencia que los demás niños. Hay varias razones por las cuales su hijo puede ser susceptible a los accidentes. Su hijo es impulsivo y puede hacer cosas como echarse a la calle sin antes averiguar si vienen coches. Su hijo parece no tener ningun temor al saltar del techo o de la terraza si alguien se lo propene. También se puede comer or beber algo venenoso. Necesita usted saber lo que está haciendo su hijo a cada momento. Tome un poco de tiempo para asegurarse que su casa y jardín estan seguros y "a prueba de chicos."

1. Vigile a su hijo cuando esta jugando afuera. Quite el vidrio, piedras, y otros objetos peligrosos del patio. Guarde o fije los basureros. Pídales a los vecinos que vigilen a su niño también.

2. Encierre con llave los medicamentos, artículos de limpieza, y otros venenos en un lugar muy seguro.

3. Cubra todos los enchufes electricos.

4. Peque calcomanias grandes sobre las puertas deslizables de vidrio.

5. Si tiene alberca, asegurese que esté bien encerrada. Nunca deje a su niño solo dentro del área de la alberca.

6. Proteja los objetos de valor. Coloque figuras de cristal, la porcelana, y la joyería fuera del alcanze de su hijo.

7. Ponga alambreras con cerradura en cada ventana para evitar caídas.

8. Ate bien las cuerdas de cortinas y persianas. No deje que cuelguen sueltas.

9. Guarde aparatos electricos, cuchillos, y herramientas en un cajón con cerradura alejado de áreas en las que suele estar su hijo.

10. Segure cuerdas y alambres sueltos para que su hijo no se tropiezca.

11. Escoja juguetes duraderos.

12. Alabe a su hijo si juega bien ("¡Muy bién! ¡Ya sabes como usar las tijeras!") Llámele la atención a otros niños que están jugando bien.

Behavior Observation Cards

Number:_____

Date:_____

Child's name: _____

Behavior observed:

What preceded behavior:

What followed behavior:

Interventions used:

Number:_____

Date:_____

Child's name: _____

Behavior observed:

What preceded behavior:

What followed behavior:

Interventions used:

Tarjetas para Observar el Comportamiento

Número:_____

Fecha:_____

Nombre del niño:_____

Comportamiento observado:

Qué procedió el comportamiento:

Qué ocurrió despues del comportamiento:

Intervenciones usadas:

Número:_____

Fecha:_____

Nombre del niño:_____

Comportamiento observado:

Qué procedió el comportamiento:

Qué ocurrió despues del comportamiento:

Intervenciones usadas:

One-Minute Memo

First day jitters?
We had them too!
Here are some things to share with you!

Child's name _____

Liked to play with _____

Needed help with _____

Told us _____

Ask your child to tell you about _____

Tomorrow _____

Signed _____

One-Minute Memo

Here are some things to share with you!

Child's name _____

Liked to play with _____

Needed help with _____

Told us _____

Ask your child to tell you about _____

Tomorrow _____

Signed _____

Recordatorio Rápido

¿Nervios?
¡Nosotros también!
¡Aquí siguen algunas cosas que queriamos decir!

Nombre del niño _____

Le gustó jugar con _____

Necesitó ayuda con _____

Nos dijo _____

Pídale a su hijo que le diga acerca de _____

Mañana _____

Firmado _____

Recordatorio Rápido

¡Aquí siguen algunas cosas que queriamos decir!

Nombre del niño _____

Le gustó jugar con _____

Necesitó ayuda con _____

Nos dijo _____

Pídale a su hijo que le diga acerca de _____

Mañana _____

Firmado _____

Chapter 8

The Role of the Computer

Computers, like all tools, must be evaluated in the context of developmentally appropriate curriculum goals (National Association for the Education of Young Children 1986). It is essential to integrate the computer into the classroom using educational principles. Thus, the computer becomes only one of a host of age-appropriate learning activities within the classroom environment. Goldstein and Jones (1998) point out that although educational software has been designed to meet these criteria and anecdotally is reported as working well with ADHD children, research in this area is very limited. It has been suggested that computer-assisted instruction that is self-paced provides immediate and frequent opportunities for responding. Also, use of consistent correction procedures may be quite beneficial for children with ADHD (Budoff, Thormann, and Gras 1984). Such instruction may be stimulating and motivating at a much higher rate than typical seat-work activities. However, thus far there has not been any definite research to suggest that the computer actually enhances either classroom behavior or on-task skills, or that children are able to transfer the skills learned to other situations. Nevertheless, the field of computer technology is such a part of today's world that it certainly holds great promise.

Parents and educators working with children who have ADHD often report that the children are extremely interested in computers (or, for that matter, any video-related activity). Parents relate that although their children have difficulty sitting still in school for a variety of tasks, they are capable of sitting with sustained attention in front of a video game or computer screen for longer periods of time. Computers, interactive CDs, and video games may interest children who have ADD for several reasons:

1. Children with ADHD respond best to activities that provide *brevity, variety,* and *structure.* Video games provide brevity because they contain short sequences with a minimum of delay. Novel and highly interesting software provides variety. At the same time, computer software operates within a structured format with a clear operating routine and a beginning and end to each activity.

2. Often these children are visual learners who respond well to the highly visual stimuli of video games and graphics programs.

3. Children with ADHD need constant and immediate reinforcement. Certain software contains a behavior component to provide immediate reinforcement for a child who is learning a new skill. The programs are structured to review the same material until the child has mastered the task. If the child needs more time to review the material on the screen, the response time can be adjusted. Software offers self-paced activities that guide the child to develop independent work skills and motivate the child to persevere.

4. The highly tactile involvement of finger to key can be rewarding to some children who have a need for kinesthetic reinforcement.

5. Margolies (1990) suggests that many children with ADHD maintain an illusory view of the world in which they are omnipotent. They may have a variety of related fantasies as self-protective strategies. Video and computer technology—especially video games and interactive CDs—provide a fantasy world in which the child can control and feel invulnerable.

In *Educational Care* (1994), author Mel Levine notes: "The computer stresses recognition memory rather than retrieval. For many children, recognition is less of a drain on memory" (194). Some authors have suggested that one benefit of the computer is that during the time the students were using the computer, the teacher was free to work with other students (Goldstein and Jones 1998; Fitzgerald, et al. 1986). Certainly many authors agree that young children approach the computer learning experience with confidence and enjoyment (Binder and Ledger 1985). Preschoolers working in pairs at the computer showed greater enjoyment and task involvement, but not better achievement, than those working alone. Such findings suggest that teachers need to continually monitor the interplay of curricular demands, instructional strategies, and children's competencies (Clements and Nastasi 1992).

Selecting Software

Software selection is one of the most important components in creating a child-oriented computer curriculum. Appropriately designed software can engender social interaction, academic skills, and a positive attitude toward the computer experience. When selecting software for children with ADHD, look for programs that provide variety, self-paced activities, and immediate reinforcement. Software that is open-ended and controlled by the child creates different environments for learning than does drill-and-practice software; it also has different social and motivational effects (Clements and Nastasi 1992). The operating procedures should be straightforward, and selective attention is particularly useful.

Resources: Computer Information

Software Information

Cambridge Development Laboratory
214 3rd Avenue
Waltham, MA 02154
(800) 637-0047
In Massachusetts: (617) 890-4640
   Special Times (computer catalog for
   special education software)

Educational Resources Information
   Center (ERIC)
2440 Research Blvd., Suite 550
Rockville, MD 20850
(800) 873-3742

High Scope Press
600 N. River Street
Ypsilanti, MI 48197
(313) 485-2000
   Survey of Early Childhood Software

Innotek, A Division of the National
   Lekotek Center
2100 Ridge Avenue
Evanston, IL 60204
(312) 328-0661

Special Education Software Center
LINC Resources, Inc.
4820 Indianola Ave.
Columbus, OH 43214
(614) 885-5599

Technical Resource Center
3200 1202 5th St., SW
Calgary, Alberta
Canada, P2R0Y6
(403) 262-9445

Video

Computers and ADD/LD (1997)
A. I. Media
P.O. Box 333
Chelsea, MI 48118

Selected Software for Young Children with ADHD

Broderbind, Inc.
17 Paul Drive
San Rafael, CA 94903
(415) 492-3500
   The Playroom®

Exceptional Children's Software, Inc.
P.O. Box 487
Hays, KS 67601
(913) 625-9281
   Run, Rabbit, Run™

Laureate Learning Systems
110 East Spring Street
Winooski, VT 05404
(802) 655-4755
   Concentrate

The Learning Company
6493 Kaiser Drive
Fremont, CA 94555
(800) 852-2255
   Reader Rabbit™
   Writer Rabbit™
   Math Rabbit™

Mindscape, Inc.
3444 Dundee Road
Northbrook, IL 60062
(800) 221-9884
   Letter Recognition and Sequencing™

Sunburst Communications
101 Castleton Street
P.O. Box 100
Pleasantville, NY 10570-0100
(800) 321-7511
   A to ZAP!™
   Memory Building Blocks™
   Muppetville™
   1, 2, 3, Sequence Me™
   Tiger's Tales™

And For the Future, When They Begin to Learn to Type!

Sunburst Communications
101 Castleton Street
P.O. Box 100
Pleasantville, NY 10570-0100
(800) 321-7511
   Type to Learn™: *Third through Eighth Grade*

Considerations When Reviewing Software

1. Is the software consistent with sound educational principles?

2. Is the software visually exciting and appealing enough to capture the child's interest?

3. Is the program self-paced?

4. Are there animated pictures or instructions to give the child on-screen guidance?

5. Can the level of difficulty be adjusted in response to the child's reaction?

6. Is it easy for the child to enter and exit the program?

7. Can each of the program's functions be controlled with just one key press?

Introducing the Computer and Software

1. Introduce the computer through short, visual activities to stimulate children's interest.

   Hands-on Example

   Using a commercially available plastic film drawing slate, show children how writing with a stylus produces a drawing on the acetate sheet. Encourage the children to experiment several times so they feel able to draw. Then lift the film to illustrate how the marks are erased.

   Next, introduce a handle-operated drawing slate (such as an Etch-A-Sketch®). Demonstrate how the children are able to create their own drawings by moving the control knobs.

   These activities will help the children understand that they are in control of making the drawing, even though the process may seem remote and magical.

2. Place the computer in one of the discovery centers in the classroom. Precede any lesson on the computer by using manipulatives to illustrate the concepts taught in the software.

   Hands-on Example

   Before introducing a software program reviewing shapes, provide opportunities to manipulate shapes in a variety of media. Encourage the children to play with puzzle forms in the shapes of circles, squares, and triangles or to make geometric shapes using stencils. Discuss how these manipulatives relate to the shapes on the computer screen.

3. To promote social interaction and provide role models, place two or three children at the computer at one time. Place the active child in the center of the group, where there is a direct view of the screen.

   Hands-on Example

   Cut out the outline of a computer, and glue it on a tongue depressor. Place it in the lap of the child who will be first. This child may then start the computer. When this child's turn is finished, the computer outline is handed to the next student. This will help everyone remember whose turn it is, especially the children who are distracted by the machine and forget the social rules.

4. Introduce a basic piece of software, such as *The Playroom*®. This writing program is designed for young children. It features oversized letters, simple operation, and speech synthesis capabilities.

5. You may want to place removable stickers on the keys that operate a particular program. A keyboard overlay to block out keys that are nonfunctional in a program is also helpful.

6. Make a picture guide that shows step by step how to operate the program. Post it next to the computer. Have the child review each step verbally with you before booting the computer.

7. At the end of the activity, review the key points of the program, and offer the child a choice of activities to explore next. Ask what the child learned on the computer, thus preparing the child for the next computer experience.

8. Keep records of the children's experiences on the computer. Record which children have had an opportunity to use the computer, the software they used, and approximately how long each child spent at the computer. A certificate of completion or printed sheet provides positive reinforcement for the child to take home.

Letter to Parents

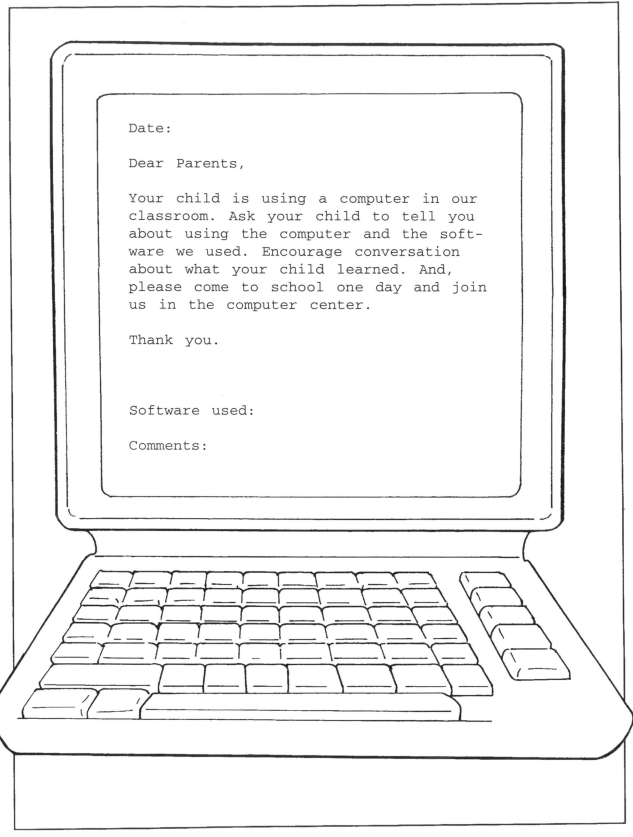

Date:

Dear Parents,

Your child is using a computer in our classroom. Ask your child to tell you about using the computer and the software we used. Encourage conversation about what your child learned. And, please come to school one day and join us in the computer center.

Thank you.

Software used:

Comments:

Carta a los Padres

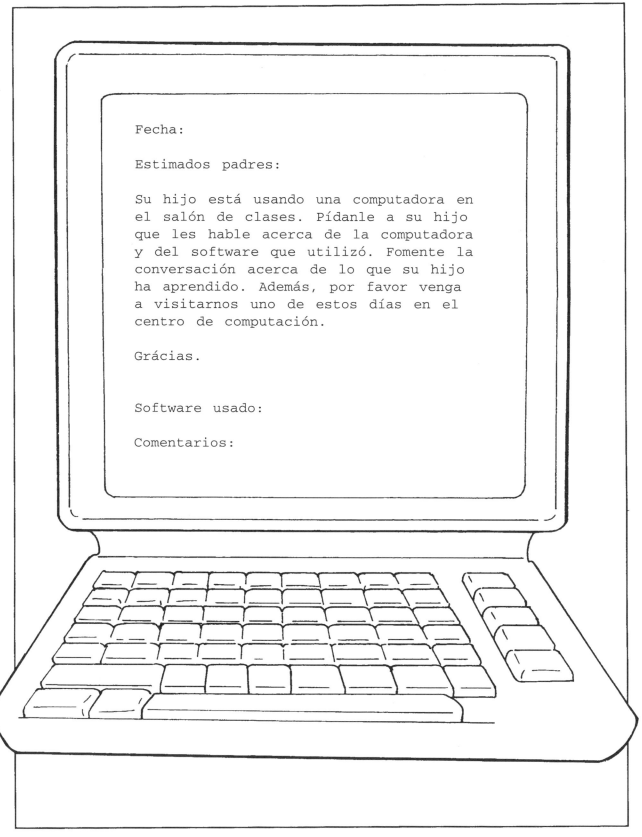

Fecha:

Estimados padres:

Su hijo está usando una computadora en el salón de clases. Pídanle a su hijo que les hable acerca de la computadora y del software que utilizó. Fomente la conversación acerca de lo que su hijo ha aprendido. Además, por favor venga a visitarnos uno de estos días en el centro de computación.

Grácias.

Software usado:

Comentarios:

References

Achenbach, T. M., and C. S. Edelbrock. 1983. *Child behavior checklist and revised child behavior profile.* Burlington: Department of Psychiatry, University of Vermont.

_____. 1986. *Teacher report form and the child behavior profile.* Burlington: Department of Psychiatry, University of Vermont.

Ackerman, D. 1990. The power of touch. *Parade.* March 25, 1990.

American Occupational Therapy Association. 1989. *Guidelines for occupational therapy services in the school system.* Rockville, MD: Author.

American Psychiatric Association. 1994. *Diagnostic and statistical manual of mental disorders (DSM-IV).* 4th ed. Washington, DC: Author.

Ayres, J. 1979. *Sensory integration and the child.* Los Angeles: Western Psychological Services.

Bailey, D., and M. Wolery. 1984. *Teaching infants and preschoolers with handicaps.* Columbus, OH: Charles E. Merrill.

Baker, J. J., and D. P. Cantwell. 1987. A prospective psychiatric follow-up of children with speech/language disorders. *Journal of American Academy of Child Psychiatry* 26:546–53.

Barkley, R. A. 1981. *Hyperactive children: A handbook for diagnosis and treatment.* New York: Guilford Press.

_____. 1987. *Defiant children: A clinician's manual for parent training.* New York: Guilford Press.

_____. 1988. The effects of methylphenidate on the interactions of preschool ADHD children with their mothers. *Journal of American Academy of Child and Adolescent Psychiatry* 27:336–41.

_____. 1990. *Attention deficit hyperactivity disorder.* New York: Guilford Press.

_____. 1997. The management of Attention Deficit Disorder. Keynote Address, Seventh Annual Attention Deficit/Hyperactivity Disorder Conference, February 20. Phoenix, AZ.

Barkley, R., G. DuPaul, and B. McMurray. 1991. A comprehensive evaluation of Attention Deficit Disorder with and without hyperactivity defined by research criteria. *Journal of Consulting and Clinical Psychology* 3:213–44.

Barkley, R., and E. Mash, eds. 1996. *Child Psychopathology,* New York: Guilford Press.

Bayley, N. 1993. *Bayley scales of infant development.* 2d ed. San Antonio: The Psychological Corporation.

Beach, S. A. 1996. I can read my own story!—Becoming literate in the primary grades. *Young Children* 52(1):22–27.

Beery, K., and N. A. Buktenica. 1997. *The developmental test of visual motor integration (Beery VMI)—Revised.* Cleveland, OH: Modern Curriculum Press.

Bender, L. 1989. *Visual-Motor Gestalt Test and its clinical use.* New York: American Orthopsychiatric Association.

Berk, L., and A. Winsler. 1995. *Scaffolding children's learning: Vygotsky and early childhood education.* Washington, DC: National Association for the Education of Young Children.

Berk, L. D., and S. Landau. 1993. Private speech of language-delayed and normally achieving children in classroom academic and laboratory context. *Child Development* 64:556–71.

Berk, L. E., and M. K. Potts. 1991. Development and functional significance of private speech among attention hyperactive disordered and normal boys. *Journal of Abnormal Psychology* 19:357–77.

Binder, S. L., and B. Ledger. 1985. *Preschool computer project report.* Oakville, Ontario: Sheridan College.

Borstelmann, L. J. 1983. Children before psychology. In *Handbook of child psychology,* edited by P. H. Mussen. New York: John Wiley and Sons.

Bower, B. 1988. Hyperactivity, the family factor. *Science News* 6:399.

Bower, G. 1976. Experiments on story understanding and recall. *Quarterly Journal of Experimental Psychology* 28:511–34.

Boyer, E. 1995. *The basic school: A community of learners*. Princeton, NJ: Carnegie Fourndation for the Advancement of Teaching.

Brigance, A. 1991. *Brigance diagnostic inventories*. North Bellerica, MA: Curriculum Associates.

Bronson, M. 1996. *The right stuff for children birth to eight: Selecting play materials to support development*. Washington DC: National Association for the Education of Young Children.

Bruner, J. S., A. Jolly, and K. Sylva, eds. 1976. *Play: Its role in development and evolution*. New York: Basic.

Buckleitner, W. 1989. *Survey of early childhood software*. Ypsilanti, MI: High Scope Press.

Budoff, M., J. Thormann, and A. Gras. 1984. *Microcomputers in special education*. Cambridge, MA: Brookline Books.

Bzoch, K. R., and R. League. 1978. *Receptive-expressive emergent language scale—Revised (REEL-R)*. Austin, TX: PRO-ED.

Campbell, S. B. 1985. Hyperactivity in preschoolers: Correlates and prognostic implications. *Clinical Psychology Review* 5:405–28.

_____. 1990. *Behavioral problems in preschoolers: Clinical and developmental issues*. New York: Guilford Press.

Carrow, E. 1990. *Test of auditory comprehension of language—Revised (TACL-R)*. Allen, TX: DLM Teaching Resources.

Castellanos, F. X. 1997. Approaching a scientific understanding of what happens in the brain in ADHD. *Attention* 4(1):30–35.

Catts, H., and A. Kamhi. 1986. The linguistic basis of reading disorders: Implications for the speech-language pathologist. *Language, Speech and Hearing Services in the Schools* 17:329–41.

Cermak, S. 1988. The relationship between attention deficit and sensory integration disorders. *Sensory Integration Special Interest Newsletter* 11(3):3–4.

Chomsky, C. 1972. Stages in language development and learning. *Harvard Educational Review* 42:1–33.

Clements, D. H., and B. K. Nastasi. 1992. Young children and computers: Crossroads and directions from research. *Young Children* 48(2):56–65.

Cohen D. 1968. The effect of literature on vocabulary and reading achievement. *Elementary English* 45:209–13, 217.

Cohen, R., L. Polsgrove, H. Reith, and J. R. K. Heinan. 1981. Evaluation of the relative effectiveness of methylphenidate and cognitive behavior modification in the treatment of kindergarten-age hyperactive children. *Journal of Abnormal Child Psychology* 9:43–54.

Conners, C. K. 1989. *Conners teacher rating scales*. Toronto: Multi-Health Systems.

_____. 1997. *Conners parent rating scale—Revised*. Toronto: Multi-Health Systems.

Cook, R., A. Tessier, and V. Armbruster. 1987. *Adapting early childhood curricula for children with special needs*. Columbus, OH: Charles E. Merrill.

Cooke, J., and D. Williams. 1987. *Working with children's language*. Tucson, AZ: Communication Skill Builders.

Degler, S. K. 1979. Putting words into wordless books. *Reading Teacher* 32(4):399–402.

DiSimoni, F. 1975. *Token test for children*. Hingham, MA: Teaching Resources.

Douglas, V. I. 1983. Attentional and cognitive problems. In *Developmental neuropsychiatry*, edited by N. M. Rudder, 280–329. New York: Guilford Press.

Douglas, V. I., and K. G. Peters. 1979. Toward a clear definition of attentional deficits of hyperactive children. In *Attention and Cognitive Development*, edited by N. G. A. Hale and M. Lewis, 173–247. New York: Plenum Press.

Downs, M. P. 1975. Hearing loss: Definition, epidemiology, and prevention. *Public Health Review* 4:255–380.

Dunn, L., and L. Dunn. 1997. *Peabody picture vocabulary test—Revised (PPVT-R3)*. Circle Pines, MN: American Guidance Service.

DuPaul, G., M. Rapport, and L. M. Perriello. 1990. *Teacher ratings of academic performance: The development of the academic performance rating scale*. Worcester, MA: Department of Psychiatry, Worcester State University.

DuPaul, G., and G. Stoner. 1994. *ADHD in the Schools*. New York: Guilford Press.

Durkin, D. 1966a. *Children who read early*. New York: Teachers College Press.

_____. 1966b. *Children who read early: Two longitudinal studies*. New York: Teachers College Press.

Ebaugh, F. G. 1923. Neuropsychiatric sequelae of acute epidemic encephalitis in children. *American Journal of Diseases of Children*. 25:89–97.

Elkind, D. 1993. *Images of the young child: Collected essays on development and education*. Washington, DC: National Association for the Education of Young Children.

Feagans, L., M. Sanyal, F. Henderson, A. Collier, and M. Appelbaum. 1987. Relationship of middle ear disease in early childhood to later narrative and attention skills. *Journal of Pediatric Psychology* 12(4):581–94.

Fitzgerald, D., B. Fick, and S. Melich. 1986. Computer-assisted instruction for students with attentional difficulties. *Journal of Learning Disabilities* 19:376.

Garber, S. W., M. D. Garber, and R. F. Spizman. 1996. *Beyond Ritalin*. New York: Villard Books.

Gibson, E. J. 1969. *The principles of perceptual learning and development*. New York: Appleton.

Goldstein S., and M. Goldstein. 1990. *Managing attention disorders in children*. New York: John Wiley and Sons.

Goldstein, S., and C. Jones. 1998. *Managing attention disorders*. Revised. New York: John Wiley and Sons.

Hagerman, R., and A. Falkenstein. 1987. An association between recurrent otitis media in infancy and later hyperactivity. *Clinical Pediatrics* 5:253–57.

Hamlett, K. W., D. S. Pellegrini, and C. K. Conners. 1987. An investigation of executive processes in the problem-solving of attention deficit disorder hyperactive children. *Journal of Pediatric Psychology* 12:227–40.

Hammill, D. D. 1985. *Detroit tests of learning aptitude*. 2d ed. Austin, TX: PRO-ED.

Hartlage, L., and C. F. Telzrow. 1986. *Neuropsychological assessment and intervention with children and adolescents*. Sarasota, FL: Sarasota Professional Resource Exchange.

Hasenstab, M. 1987. *Language learning and otitis media*. Boston: Little, Brown.

Hepworth, J., C. Jones, and C. Sehested. 1991. Teacher survey of ADHD in Arizona third- and fourth-grade children. Unpublished research study. College of Nursing, Arizona State University.

Hiresko, W. P., D. K. Reid, and D. Hammill. 1981. *Test of early language development*. Austin, TX: PRO-ED.

Holman, M., B. Banet, and D. P. Weikart. 1979. *Young children in action*. Ypsilanti, MI: High Scope Press.

Howard, J., L. Beckwith, C. Rodnig, and V. Kropenski. 1989. The development of young children of substance-abusing parents: Insights from seven years of intervention and research. *Zero to Three: Bulletin of National Center for Clinical Infant Programs* 9(5):8–12.

Ingersoll, B., and S. Goldstein. 1993. *Attention deficit disorder and learning disabilities*. New York: Doubleday.

Jones, C. B. 1989a. Teachers' corner. In *Kids getting you down?* (Newsletter). San Diego: Learning Development Services.

_____. 1989b. Managing the difficult child. *Family Day Caring* (Nov/Dec):6–7.

———. 1993. *Surrogate parent training manual*. Phoenix: Arizona Department of Education, Special Education Division.

———. 1994. *Attention deficit disorder: Strategies for school-age children*. San Antonio, TX: The Psychological Corporation.

Kagan, J. 1964. *Matching familiar figures test*. Unpublished manuscript. Harvard University.

Katz, M. 1997. *On playing a poor hand well*. New York: W. W. Norton.

Kaufman, A. S., and N. Kaufman. 1983. *The Kaufman assessment battery for children: Interpretive manual*. Circle Pines, MN: American Guidance Service.

Kavale, K., and D. Mattson. 1983. One jumped off the balance beam: Meta-analysis of perceptual-motor training. In *Annual review of learning disabilities: A journal of learning disabilities reading,* vol. 1, edited by G. Senf and J. Toreson, 118–26. Chicago: Professional Press.

Lambert, N. M., J. Sandoval, and D. Sassone. 1978. Prevalence of hyperactivity in elementary school children as a function of social system definers. *American Journal of Orthopsychiatry* 48:446–63.

Landau, S., R. Milich, and T. A. Widiger. 1991. Conditional probabilities of child interview symptoms in the diagnosis of attention deficit disorder. *Journal of Child Psychology and Psychiatry* 32:501–13.

Lerner, J. 1988. *Learning disabilities: Theories, diagnosis, and teaching strategies*. Boston: Houghton Mifflin.

Levine, M. 1981. *The ANSER system: Aggregate neurobehavioral student health and education review*. Cambridge, MA: Educators Publishing Service.

———. 1987a. Attention deficits: The diverse effects of weak control systems in childhood. *Pediatric Annals* 16(2):117–30.

———. 1987b. *Developmental variation and learning disorders*. Cambridge, MA: Educators Publishing Service.

———. 1994. *Educational care*. Cambridge, MA: Educators Publishing Service.

Lewinsohn, P. M., M. Hops, H. Roberts, B. E. Seeley, J. R. Andrews, and J. A. Andrews. 1993. Adolescent psychopathology: I. Prevalence and incidence of depression and other DSM-III-R disorders in high school students. *Journal of Abnormal Psychology,* 21:133–44.

Love, A. J., and M. G. G. Thompson. 1988. Language disorders and attention deficit disorders in young children referred for psychiatric service: Analysis of prevalence and a conceptual synthesis. *American Journal of Orthopsychiatry* 58(1):52–64.

Margolies, B. 1990. Attention deficit and the Macintosh. *Macintosh Lab Monitor* 9:11–13.

McCarney, S. B. 1989. *Attention deficit disorders intervention manual*. Columbia, MO: Hawhorne Educational Services.

McLane, J. B., and G. D. McNamee. 1990. *Early literacy*. Cambridge, MA: Harvard University Press.

Minde, K., D. Lewn, G. Weiss, H. Labigueeur, D. I. Douglas, and E. Sykes. 1971. The hyperactive child in elementary school: A five-year follow-up study. *Exceptional Children* 38:215–21.

Mirsky, A. F. 1978. Attention: A neuropsychological perspective. *Education and the brain,* edited by J. S. Shall and A. F. Mirsky, 33–60. Chicago: National Society for the Study of Education.

Morrow, L. M., and J. K. Smith. 1990. The effect of group sizes on interactive storybook reading. *Reading Research Quarterly* 25:213–31.

National Association for the Education of Young Children. 1986. Position statement on developmentally appropriate practice in early childhood programs serving children through age 8. *Young Children* 41(6):3–19.

Oetter, P. 1986. Sensory integration approach to the treatment of attention deficit disorders. *Sensory Integration Special Interest Newsletter* 9:2.

Rapoport, J. 1995. *New findings in brain development in children with ADHD*. Seventh Annual Conference, Children and Adults with Attention Deficit Disorder (CH.A.D.D.), Washington DC.

Resnak, R. 1979. *The brain: The last frontier*. New York: Warner Books.

Reynell, J. 1980. *Language development*. Lancaster, England: M.T.P. Press.

Rowe, K. J., and K. S. Rowe. 1992. The relationship between inattentiveness in classroom and reading achievement. Part B: An explanatory study. *Journal of the American Academy of Child and Adolescent Psychiatry* 31:357–68.

Royeen, D. B., and D. Marsh. 1988. Promoting occupational therapy in the schools. *American Journal of Occupational Therapy* 42(11):713–17.

Scaldwell, W. A., and J. E. Frame. 1985. Prevalence of otitis media in Cree and Ojibway school children in six Ontario communities. *Journal of American Indian Education* 25:1–5.

Searight, H., J. Nahlik, and D. Campbell. 1995. Attention deficit? Hyperactivity disorder assessment, diagnosis, and management. *The Journal of Family Practice* 40(3):270–78.

Secord, G., J. Erickson, M. Bush, and T. Bush. 1988. Neuropsychological sequelae of otitis media in children and adolescents with learning disabilities. *Journal of Pediatric Psychology* 13(4):531–42.

Shaywitz, B. A. 1987. *The Yale children's inventory*. New Haven, CT: Yale University Medical School.

Shaywitz, S. E., J. M. Fletcher, and B. A. Shaywitz. 1994. Issues in the definition and classification of attention deficit disorder. *Topics in Language Disorders* 14:1–25.

Shaywitz, S. E., and B. A. Shaywitz. 1991. Introduction to the special series on attention deficit disorder. *Journal of Learning Disabilities* 24(2):68–71.

Silver, L. B. 1989. Learning disabilities. *Journal of the American Academy of Child and Adolescent Psychiatry* 20:309–13.

_____. 1990. Attention deficit-hyperactivity disorder: Is it a learning disability or a related disorder? *Journal of Learning Disabilities* 23(7):394–97.

Social Integration Project. 1989. *Let's be social: Language-based social skills for preschool at-risk children*. Tucson, AZ: Communication Skill Builders.

Strickland, D. S., and D. Taylor. 1989. Family storybook reading: Implications for children, families and curriculum. In *Emerging literacy: Young children learn to read and write*, edited by D. S. Strickland and L. M. Morrow. Newark, DE: International Reading Association.

Stump, J. 1992. *Our best hope: Early intervention with prenatally drug-exposed infants and their families*. Washington, DC: Child Welfare League of America.

Tant, J. L., and V. I. Douglas. 1982. Problem solving in hyperactive, normal, and reading-disabled boys. *Journal of Abnormal Psychology* 10:285–306.

Teale, W. 1978. Positive environments for learning to read: What studies of early readers tell us. *Language Arts* 55:922–32.

Telzrow, C. F., and B. Speer. 1986a. Learning disabled children: General suggestions for maximizing instruction. *Techniques: A Journal for Remedial Education and Counseling* 2:341–52.

_____. 1986b. Neuropsychologically based learning disorders: Implications for instruction. *Techniques: A Journal for Remedial Education and Counseling* 2:230–47.

Ullmann, R. K., E. K. Sleator, and R. K. Sprague. 1985. *Add-H comprehensive teacher's rating scale (ACTeRS)*. Champaign, IL: Meri Tech.

_____. 1997. *Add-H comprehensive parent rating scale*. Champaign, IL: Meri Tech.

Viadero, D. 1989. Drug-exposed babies pose special problems. *Education Week* 9(3):1–11.

Wechsler, D. 1991. *Wechsler preschool and primary scale of intelligence—Revised. (WPPSI)*. San Antonio: The Psychological Corporation.

_____. 1991. *Wechsler intelligence scale for children—3d ed. (WISC-III)*. San Antonio: The Psychological Corporation.

Weiss, G. 1990. Prevalence of learning disabilities. *New England Journal of Medicine* (20):1414–15.

Weiss, G., and L. Heichman. 1986. *Hyperactive children grown up.* New York: Guilford Press.

Wender, P. 1987. *The hyperactive child, adolescent and adult: Attention deficit disorder through the life span.* New York: Oxford University Press.

Winsler, A. 1994. *The social origins and self-regulatory quality of private speech in hyperactive and normal children.* Ph.D. dissertation. Stanford University.

Woodcock, R., and M. Bonner Johnson. 1989. *Woodcock-Johnson Psychoeducational Battery—Revised.* Allen, TX: DLM Teaching Resources.

Zametkin, A., T. Nordahl, M. Gross, C. King, W. Semple, J. Rumsey, S. Hamburger, and R. Cohen. 1990. Cerebral glucose metabolism in adults with hyperactivity of childhood onset. *The New England Journal of Medicine* 323(20):1361–66.

Zeanah, C., and S. McDonough. 1989. *Clinical approaches to families in early intervention.* Seminars in Perinatology. 123(6):35–38.

Zentall, S. S. 1985a. A context for hyperactivity. In *Advances in learning and behavioral disabilties.* Vol. 4, edited by K. D. Gadow and I. Bialer, 273–343. Greenwich, CT: JAI Press.

———. 1985b. Stimulus control factors in the search performance of hyperactive children. *Journal of Learning Disabilities* 18:480–85.

Zentall, S., and T. Kruczek. 1988. The attraction of colors for active attention-problem children. *Exceptional Children* 54(4):357–62.

Ziffer, R. 1990. Who wants to play with Jason? *Play! Magazine* 1(1):10–12.

Zimmerman, I. L, V. G. Steiner, and R. E. Pond. 1992. *Preschool language scale—3. (PLS-3).* San Antonio: The Psychological Corporation.

Additional Reading

Abilkoff, H., R. Gittelman-Klein, and D. F. Klein. 1977. Validation of a classroom observation code for hyperactive children. *Journal of Consulting and Clinical Psychology* 45:772–83.

Bauwens, J., and J. J. Hourcade. 1989. Hey, would you just listen? *Teaching the Exceptional Child* 21 (Spring):22–61.

Bee, H. 1978. *The developing child*. New York: Harper & Row.

Biessman, L., C. Jones, S. Kix, and J. Osborn. 1970. *Catalog of experiences*. Unpublished curriculum material. Richfield (MN) Public Schools.

Bratshaw, M. L., and Y. M. Peret. 1986. *Children with handicaps: A medical primer*. New York: Paul H. Brookes.

Call, J. D. 1985. *Practice of pediatrics*. Philadelphia: Harper & Row.

Carey, W., B. Carey, and S. C. McDevitt. 1978. A revision of the infant temperament questionnaire. *Pediatrics* 61:735–39.

Chall, J. 1967. *Learning to read: The great debate*. New York: McGraw-Hill.

CIBA-GEIGY Corporation, Pharmaceuticals Division. 1989. *Parents helping parents*. Summit, NJ: Author.

Comings, D. E. 1990. *Tourette's syndrome and human behavior*. Duarte: Hope Press.

Conners, C. K. 1980. *Food additives and hyperactive children*. New York: Plenum Press.

Cooper, T. L. 1976. *Skiltrac activities*. Columbus, OH: Center for Educational Intervention.

Copeland, A. P. 1979. Types of private speech produced by hyperactive and non-hyperactive boys. *Journal of Abnormal Child Psychology* 7:169–77.

Demma, C. A. 1989. School nursing management of attention deficit disorder. *School Nurse* (Oct):8–15.

Deutsch, M. 1963. The disadvantaged child and the learning process. In *Education in depressed areas*, edited by A. H. Passon, 168–78. New York: Teachers College Press.

Dunn, W. 1988. Models of occupational therapy service provision in the school system. *American Journal of Occupational Therapy* 42(11):718–23.

Edelbrock, C. 1988. *Children attention problems (CAP)*. Worcester, MA: Department of Psychiatry, Worcester State University.

Eyberg, S. M. 1980. Eyberg child behavior inventory. *Journal of Clinical Child Psychology* 9:22–28.

Forehand, F., and R. McMahon. 1981. *Helping the noncompliant child: A clinician's guide to parent training*. New York: Guilford Press.

Galvin, M. 1988. *Otto learns about his medicine: A story about medication for hyperactive children*. New York: Imagination Press.

Gessell, A., H. M. Halverson, H. Thompson, S. L. Ilg, B. N. Costner, L. B. Ames, and C. S. Matruda. 1940. *The first five years of life: A guide to the study of the preschool child*. New York: Harper & Row.

Goldstein, S., and E. Pollock. 1988 *Teacher observation checklist*. Salt Lake City: Neurology, Learning, and Behavior Center.

Gordon, M. 1983. *The Gordon diagnostic system*. Dewitt, NY: Gordon Systems.

Gruber, H. 1989. Why an association for learning disabilities should be concerned with ADD/ADHD. Association for Children with Learning Disabilities. *Newsbriefs* 1:12.

Herzog, M., and J. Gibbs. 1989. A chance to chant. *Teacher's guide*. Unpublished curriculum material. Deer Valley (AZ) School District.

Jacobs, R. G., K. D. O'Leary, and C. Rosenblad. 1978. Formal and informal classroom settings: Effects on hyperactivity. *Journal of Abnormal Child Psychology* 6:47–59.

Jones, C. B. 1986. Grandparents read to special preschoolers. *Teaching the Exceptional Child* 8 (Fall):36–37.

_____. 1987. Effect of oral reading by senior citizens on the oral language and readiness skills of language delayed pre-kindergarten children. Ph.D. dissertation, University of Akron.

Jones, C. B., and R. Melmed. 1988. Talk about attention deficits. Pilot Parents, Phoenix, AZ. *Pilot Parent Newsletter.* Spring:3–4.

Kaplan, B. J., J. McNicol, R. A. Conte, and H. K. Moghadam. 1989. Dietary replacement in preschool-aged hyperactive boys. *Pediatrics* 83:7–17.

Karnes, M. 1968. Helping young children develop language skills. *Teaching Exceptional Children* 3:220–24.

Kirk, S., T. McCarthy, and W. Kirk. 1968. *Illinois test of psycholinguistic abilities (ITPA).* Urbana: University of Illinois Press.

Levine, M. 1987. Attention deficits: The diverse effects of weak control systems in childhood. *Pediatric Annals* 16(2):117–30.

Levine, M., and N. Jordan. 1987. Learning disorders: The neurodevelopmental underpinnings. *Contemporary Pediatrics* 4:16–43.

Levine, M., and R. Melmed. 1982. The unhappy wanderers: Children with attention deficits. *Journal of Pediatric Clinics of North America* 29(1):105–20.

Mash, E. J., L. Terdal, and K. Anderson. 1973. The response class matrix: A procedure for recording parent-child interactions. *Journal of Consulting and Clinical Psychology* 40:163–64.

Mastropieri, M. 1988. Using the keyword method. *Teaching Exceptional Children* 20 (Winter):4–8.

Mongon, D., and S. Hart. 1989. *Improving classroom behavior: New directions for teachers and pupils.* New York: Teachers College Press.

Montgomery, R. 1986. *Memory made easy: The complete book of memory training.* New York: American Management Association.

Moss, D. M. 1989. *Shelly, the hyperactive turtle.* Rockville, MD: Woodbine House.

Mott, M. 1974. *Teaching the pre-academic child: Activities for children displaying difficulties of processing information.* Springfield, IL: Charles C. Thomas.

Patterson, G. R. 1982. *Coercive family process.* Eugene, OR: Castalia.

Pelham, W. E., M. S. Atkins, H. A. Murphy, and K. S. White. 1981. Operationalization and validation of attention deficit disorder. Paper presented to the Association for Advancement of Behavioral Therapy, Toronto, Canada.

Piaget, J. 1964. Development and learning. In *Piaget rediscovered,* edited by I. N. Ripple and V. Rockcastle. Ithaca, NY: Cornell University Press.

Ramey, C. T., and S. I. Ramey. 1992. Effective early intervention. *Mental Retardation* 30: 337–45.

Reitan, R. M. 1984. *The Halstead Reitan lateral dominance examination.* Tucson, AZ: Reitan Neuropsychology Laboratory.

Robinson, B. 1990. The teacher's role in working with children of alcoholic parents. *Young Children* (May):68–73.

Salend, S. J. 1990. *Effective mainstreaming.* New York: Macmillan.

Sandoval, J., N. Lambert, and D. M. Sassone. 1981. The comprehensive treatment of hyperactive children: A continuing problem. *Journal of Learning Disabilities* 14:117–18.

Sehested, C. 1989. *General principles for sensory motor activities.* Photocopied course material. College of Nursing, Arizona State University.

Shaywitz, S. E., and B. A. Shaywitz. 1988. Attention deficit disorder: Current perspectives. In *Learning disabilities: Proceeding of the national conference 1988,* edited by J. F. Kavanough and T. J. Truss, 369–523. Parkton, MD: York Press.

Steward, M. A., B. T. Thatch, and M. R. Freidin. 1970. Accidental poisoning in the hyperactive child syndrome. *Diseases of the Nervous System* 31:403–07.

Swanson, J. M., A. Barlow, and M. Kinsbourne. 1979. Task specificity of responses to stimulant drugs in laboratory tests. *Capital International Journal of Mental Health* 8:67–82.

Thomas, A., and S. Chess. 1977. *Temperament and development.* New York: Brunner/Mazel.

Waldrop, M. S., and C. F. Halverson. 1971. Minor physical anomalies and hyperactive behavior in young children. In *The Exceptional Infant,* edited by I. Hellmuth, 343–80. New York: Brunner/Mazel.

Watson, J. A., R. E. Nida, and D. D. Shade. 1986. Educational issues concerning young children and microcomputers: Lego with Logo? *Early Childhood Development and Care* 23:294–316.

Wender, P. 1971. *Minimal brain dysfunction in children.* New York: Wiley-Interscience.

Whalen, C. K., B . E. Collins, B. Henker, S. R. Alkus, D. Adams, and S. Stapp. 1978. Behavior observations of hyperactive children and methylphenidate effects in systematically structured classroom environments: Now you see them, now you don't. *Journal of Pediatric Psychology* 3:177–84.

Wolery, M. P., S. Strain, and D. B. Bailey. 1992. Reaching potentials of children with special needs. In *Reading potentials: Appropriate curriculum and assessment for young children.* Vol. 1, edited by S. Bredekamp and T. Rosegrant, 95. Washington DC: National Association for the Education of Young Children.

Zentall, S. S. 1985. Stimulus control factors in the search performance of hyperactive children. *Journal of Learning Disabilities* 18:480–85.

_____. 1986. Effects of color stimulation on performance and activity of hyperactive and non-hyperactive children. *Journal of Educational Psychology* 78:159–65.

Zentall, S. S., D. E. Gohs, and B. Culotta. 1983. Language and activity of hyperactive and comparison children during listening tasks. *Exceptional Children* 50:255-66.